THE KHMERS OF CAMBODIA

the story of a mysterious people

THE KHMERS

THE KINGS OF CAMBODIA

OF CAMBODIA

the story of a mysterious people

BY I. G. EDMONDS

photographs by the author

THE BOBBS-MERRILL COMPANY, INC. · INDIANAPOLIS · NEW YORK

THE BOBBS-MERRILL COMPANY, INC.
A Subsidiary of Howard W. Sams & Co., Inc.
Publishers: Indianapolis / Kansas City / New York

Book design by Ragna Tischler Goddard
Map by Jack H. Fuller

to Annette,
beloved daughter

CONTENTS

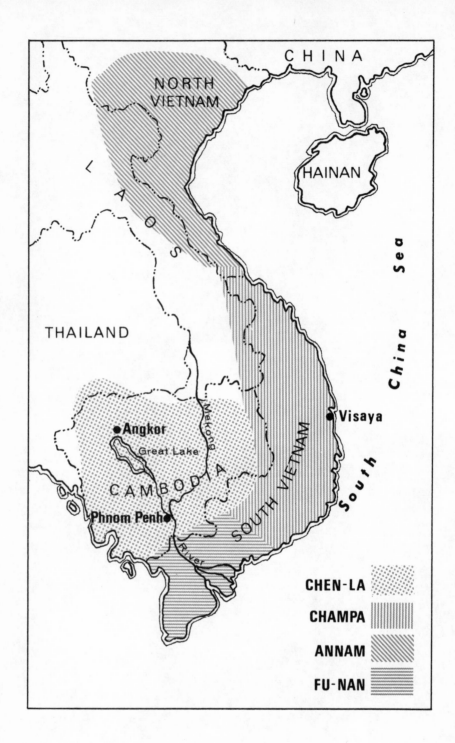

INTRODUCTION

In Indochina, squeezed between Laos, Thailand, and Vietnam, is a tiny Southeast Asian country scarcely the size of the state of Washington. This is Cambodia, the land of the Khmers (pronounced *k-mĕr's*), a strange race who came from no one knows where, built a mysterious empire, and then saw that great civilization collapse for reasons as unknown as the race's origin.

For the last 105 years Cambodia has been a country scarcely known to the western world. It was too small and too remote to receive much notice. If mentioned at all, it was usually in connection with the strange and wonderful lost city found in its jungles by the French naturalist Henri Mouhot in 1860.

This fabulous city, Angkor Thom, is generally acknowledged to be one of the wonders of the modern world. However, before the prevalence of air travel after World War II, only the most hardy travelers dared make the extremely difficult trip into the deep jungles to see these strange ruins. Thus, the western world heard of Cambodia only from an occasional travel book and a few magazine articles.

Suddenly all this changed. Cambodia is now regularly in the headlines, diplomats accord it serious attention, and the United States Pentagon has more than a passing interest in it. The world has become interested in Cambodia because it shares a border with

Vietnam, which has caused both East and West to woo this tiny country. But in a rare display of independence, Cambodia has defied both sides.

Between 1955 and 1963 the United States poured millions of dollars into the country in foreign aid. But when Cambodia decided that the Americans were trying to influence her, she refused further aid, broke off diplomatic relations, and angrily denounced her former benefactor. After this, she seemed for a time to lean toward Communism, but when this was regarded as a "settled fact" in the West, the Cambodian government suddenly made widespread arrests of native Communist sympathizers.

Cambodia's strategic position caused western journalists and writers to take an interest in the country they had previously ignored. Aside from its strategic importance, they found a certain fascination in this land of perpetual summer and true mystery, where the ruins of Angkor Thom, the lost city, seemed part of a fantastic romance.

Each year increasing numbers of tourists travel to this strange country. Here they find one of the few places left on earth of mystery and romance, those qualities that modern civilization has stripped away from so much of the rest of the world.

CHAPTER 1

****

THE LAND
OF THE KHMERS

THE LAND OF the Khmer people is an immense jungle plain surrounded by plateaus and mountains that separate it from its Southeast Asian neighbors, Thailand, Laos, and Vietnam.

The sandstone Dangrek Mountains are between Cambodia and
Thailand, and there is a high plateau where the country borders on
Laos in the northeast. The western Thai frontier and the area where
the Gulf of Siam touches Cambodia are distinguished by the Cardomon Mountains and the vividly beautiful Elephant Range. Here
granite peaks act as a barrier to the moist air that blows in from the
Gulf of Siam. This natural barrier causes the interior of Cambodia
to have a drier, more pleasant climate than most of tropical Indochina.

About three quarters of the country lies in a vast, flat basin between these high borderlands. At one time, geologists say, this immense plain was part of the Gulf of Siam. There are two conflicting stories as to why the water turned to land. The natives claim that in the dim mists of a time long past, a handsome prince came in a boat rowed by 6,000 soldiers. The prince sailed across the gulf that is now the land of the Khmers. One evening he saw on the shore the most beautiful woman who ever lived, and they fell in love. However, she was not a real woman. She was the beloved daughter of the *naga* king. The naga is the deadly hooded cobra of Asia, and the king is a tremendous serpent with seven hooded heads who ruled all the land surrounding the water where Cambodia now stands. The snake king did not approve of his daughter's love for a mortal man. His regard for her was so great, however, that he reluctantly gave permission for the marriage. In order to provide the prince and the princess with a land to rule, the great snake with the seven heads drank all of the water in the gulf, thereby creating the land we now know as Cambodia. The lovers settled there as king and queen and lived happily ever after to become the father and mother of the Khmers.

The other account of Cambodia's origin comes from geologists, who trace its beginnings back to the Paleozoic era when the giant reptiles were first making their appearance on earth. Thus, perhaps in their own way geologists are verifying the native tale of the ancient snake king.

During this era there was a giant submarine earthquake, which raised a vast plateau under the Cambodian gulf and produced a very shallow sea. Emptying into this sea was the Mekong River. It is one of the longest rivers in the world with headwaters in China's Szechwan province, which is also the source of Burma's Salween River, China's Yangtze, and India's Brahmaputra.

In its long fall out of the Chinese highlands, the Mekong River carried with it an immense amount of silt which it deposited in the gulf for the next 200 million years. This alluvial deposit gradually filled the sea. Today the Mekong still cuts across the land it made.

Cambodian homes on the shores of Tonle Sap, the Great Lake.

After leaving China it is trapped between tremendous gorges cut through granite mountains in upper Thailand and Laos, but once the river reaches the Cambodian plain, it is free to spread out. Taking full advantage of its new freedom, it has become as important to the lives of the Khmers of Cambodia as the Nile is to the people of Egypt.

In some places the river is three miles wide and so deep that ocean-going vessels can sail upriver for 200 miles to the capital, Phnom Penh (pronounced *pnom pen'*). At Phnom Penh, the Mekong joins the Tonle Sap (Great Lake) River and the Brassaq River to form what the Khmers call the "four arms of the river." Here the Tonle Sap joins the Mekong in a curious partnership that is the key to the Khmer prosperity. From November until June the Mekong is swollen by torrential floods from water it picks up in its 2,700-mile journey from its source in China. During this long rainy season the crest of the river rises as high as 50 feet. The runoff from the flood is further aggravated by heavy monsoon rains in Cambodia. The river cannot accommodate the tremendous mass of water, and the surplus is pushed up the Tonle Sap River and into the Tonle Sap, or Great Lake. Normally this lake is about 100 square miles in size and not over five feet deep, but the overflow from the flooding Mekong swells it to 770 square miles. The lake overflows, washing across thousands of rice paddies and into the thick jungles of Central Cambodia.

Like the Egyptian Nile, this annual flooding lays down a rich silt that fertilizes the rice fields for a new harvest. The fish harvest of the lake itself is equally as important to the national economy as is the rice harvest. When the floods begin, the farmers flee to high ground, leaving their homes resting safe from the water on high-rising stilts. The lake area is practically deserted. Then, in mid-November, the flooding Mekong starts to drop. Water in the swollen lake begins to flow back down the Tonle Sap. The change is a signal for 30,000 fishermen to rush to the lake. Rattan dams and fish traps are hastily put in place. Millions of fish spread over the 770 square miles of water are squeezed down into the normal 100-mile area.

These boats, called sampans, are the Cambodians' water trucks and taxis. At a lake waterfront men load cargo which will be floated to Phnom Penh for sale.

Fish are jammed so thickly about the dams that they can literally be lifted out of the water in buckets.

As the boatloads of fish are brought in, assembly lines are set up. Hundreds of sweating cleaners rip the fish open. With a quick, practiced hand the meat is separated. Some of it goes into vats to be salted, some into boats, to be rushed to the fresh-fish markets in Phnom Penh, and some to factories to be made into a popular fish paste.

The harvest, which is too large to be termed only fishing, goes on for weeks. By the end of the season the catch totals 130 million pounds, which is more than four times the salt-water fish catch by all boats operating in Cambodian waters in the Gulf of Siam. About half the catch goes to make the Khmers the best-fed natives in Southeast Asia. The rest is surplus and is exported.

When the fishermen withdraw at the end of the season, the farmers are already returning to their refertilized farms. The ground is so wet and fertile that in many places rice can be sown by hand. This eliminates the backbreaking transplanting by hand, which is one of the most characteristic sights in the Orient.

Beyond the Great Lake region the country is 90 percent timbered, ranging from deep jungle to open forest. In the jungles there are tiger, wild elephant, buffalo, and the deadly cobra. Such wild game, except for the cobra, avoids the open forest, leaving the extra-tall trees to thousands of chattering gibbons who swing through the branches like furry Tarzans.

The open forest is especially beautiful in the region north of Tonle Sap. The tall spire of the fromager tree and the gray-white trunks of giant fig trees lace their branches overhead to shut out all direct sunlight from the ground below. The light filters through in a soft green glow of almost mystic quality. There are birds by the thousands—cranes, heron, pheasant, and wild duck. Butterflies are often as large as parrots.

On the jungle plains the land rarely rises more than six feet above sea level. But as we approach the Cardomon Mountains going west toward the Gulf of Siam, the scenery changes abruptly. The land

A boy washes in a stream near a waterwheel used for irrigation.

becomes rougher. The timber is so thick that it is almost impossible to penetrate. Steep cliffs become numerous and streams plunge down them in rushing cataracts.

There is a considerable mist in the highlands that is lacking in the drier Cambodian basin. Lianas and other thick vines festoon the closely packed trees. Some of the plunging cliffs and lush vegetation remind one of the mountain regions of Hawaii. Although temperatures are lower here than in the lowland plains, Cambodia is still a land of perpetual summer. Towering above is 50,700-foot Phnom Kmock. This mountain's base rises from land only a few feet above sea level, which makes it appear much higher than it really is.

The Cambodians of Khmer stock shun this high country, clinging to the lowlands and leaving the hills to the *phnongs,* an all-inclusive word for savages which the Khmers apply indiscriminately to the six or more primitive tribes who follow their age-old ways of life in the highlands.

The Khmers are country folk, with their economy based solidly on rice and fish. In the entire nation there are only six cities of any size, and only 17 percent of the population lives in them. The rest of the population is widely scattered in rural settlements that rarely exceed a population of 200. There are thousands of these villages. Most are built near streams, for the Cambodian loves water. (It has been said that he is like the elephant: he cannot exist without his daily bath. In the evenings the entire village troops down to the water to bathe in the stream. Carvings on the walls of ancient ruins show that this same ritual has been going on for the last thousand years.)

These villages are virtually self-governing. Each has a headman who is responsible to one of the fourteen provincial governments. The governments of the provinces in turn are responsible directly to the national government in Phnom Penh. This government is a constitutional monarchy with the king as head of state and head of the national Buddhist religion. He is also supreme commander of the armed forces.

The government is firmly in Khmer hands, but the Chinese residents of the country completely dominate its economic life. Lately, the national government has expressed concern at the way the Chinese control the country's businesses. However, most of the Khmers themselves are indifferent to business, preferring to fish and farm. They are glad to leave the buying and selling to others. The average Cambodian has a high regard for the Chinese in Cambodia. The old grandmothers who arrange family marriages are especially happy when they can secure a Chinese son-in-law for the family. They know he either is rich or will be soon.

The Chinese are centered in Phnom Penh. They originally came to Cambodia from Cholon, the Chinese sector of Saigon in Vietnam. All were carefully screened by the French before being permitted to immigrate to Cambodia in order to weed out Communist sympathizers. However, the Cambodian Chinese have strong family ties in the Old Country, so they are careful not to antagonize the Red government in China. When Chou En-lai, the former Chinese premier, visited Phnom Penh several years ago, the local Chinese hastily hung out Red Chinese flags in his honor. They are very much aware that China has her hungry eyes on the vast undeveloped natural resources of Cambodia.

There are about 130,000 Chinese in Phnom Penh, a figure that is fairly accurate because urban areas are stable and can be counted. National census figures are not available for the rest of the country. Scattered villages and the mobility of the hill people make a national count impossible. What population figures there are come from estimates of foreign economic advisors. The generally accepted figure is a total population of five million, of which the Khmers make up 85 percent and the Chinese and Vietnamese 5 percent each; the remaining 5 percent is divided among Japanese, Indians, Cham-Malays, and a handful of Europeans who are mostly French holdovers from the days when Cambodia was part of French Indo-China.

There is no persecution of minority groups in Cambodia. All live in harmony together. Religion, one of the greatest sources of interracial discord, is non-existent there. Even though the 85-percent majority is solidly and devoutly Buddhist there is complete toleration of the practices of minority groups even when these constitute what the majority regards as sinful. An example is the relationship between the Cambodians and the Cham-Malays. The Chams are devout Muslims. They butcher animals freely, while Buddhists are forbidden by their religion to kill any living thing.

Although the different races get along well together, this does not necessarily mean they like each other. The Vietnamese are hated by the Khmers. The Thais are not well liked either. This is a result of heritage. For hundreds of years the Thais and the Vietnamese competed with each other in dismembering Cambodia. The long wars and national humiliations have not been forgotten. It has bred a national suspicion of all foreign countries and is the basis for Cambodia's inability to get along with any other country for long. The Cambodians are certain that foreign nations have designs on Cambodia. It must be admitted that they have historic reasons for such a belief.

To understand how this history evolved, we must go back and see how the Khmers grew out of savagery and went on to build a truly awesome and mysterious civilization which eventually collapsed, returning the Khmer people once more to a backward and primitive life.

CHAPTER 2

****

THE SONS OF KAMBU

THE ORIGIN OF the Cambodians who called themselves Khmers is uncertain. Possibly they drifted down from South China in prehistoric times. Physical evidence indicates that they are from the same folk roots as the Thais, Burmese, and the Annamites who became the Vietnamese.

The Khmer, however, is darker than the Vietnamese. He averages five feet four inches in height and has a somewhat flatter nose than either the Vietnamese or the Thai. His eyes are oval and free from the Mongolian fold, which led to an early belief, no longer held, that the Khmer originated in India. The Khmer's hair is black and he is more muscular than others of the Southeast Asian races.

When the Khmers first appeared in history they shared the region of Indochina with the Funanese and the Chams. The Khmer kingdom of Chen-la (or Tchen-la) occupied the northern half of present-day Cambodia. The Chams, ruling Champa on the east coast of what is now the north section of South Vietnam, were a caucasian race who supposedly came from India. The Funanese of Fu-nan were a native stock who had come under strong Indian influence. They occupied the present Mekong River delta area of South Vietnam.

Another important nation in Indochina at the beginning of the Christian era was Annam. The Annamites occupied the area that is now North Vietnam. Eventually they pushed southward and took all of Vietnam.

The rise of the great Chinese civilization in the northeast had little initial effect upon the primitive tribes living their nomadic lives along the Mekong River. Knowledge of bronze and, later, iron filtered down to them. They also learned the art of rice cultivation from China.

The Chinese confined their push to the north. The savages in their steamy jungles to the south did not interest them until the third century A.D. when China overran Annam.

The great civilization developing in India was more restless. By the first century A.D. Indian explorers were pushing into Southeast Asia. It was they who first brought civilization to the tribes living along the Mekong.

Cambodian history is so interwoven with legend that no attempt is made to separate the two, even in the country's schools. However, contemporary Chinese records show that in many instances there is a solid historical basis for these legends. For example, there is the story of a handsome Hindu prince who had a vision that directed him to explore the South China Sea. Taking his magic sword and a bow so strong that only he could bend it, the prince set sail in a convoy of boats rowed by sixty warriors. They worked their way along the coast of Burma, Thailand, and the Malay Archipelago before landing on the coast of Fu-nan where the Mekong splits into several mouths before emptying into the South China Sea.

Here the Hindus found a tribe so savage it had not yet learned to wear clothes. The savages, led by a beautiful queen, had apparently progressed to the point where they could make dugout canoes and fight with spears. Fearful of the strangers in their odd boats, the queen gathered her forces and attacked. Before the clumsy dugouts could close in on the Hindus, the prince bent his great bow and shot an arrow through the queen's boat. Awed by such tremendous strength, the savages fell on their knees to worship the strangers as gods. The beautiful queen fell in love with the prince, and so they were married. The prince settled with the tribe and introduced Hindu culture and worship of Siva, the Hindu god of both life and death.

The idea of a stranger coming to the land and marrying a local princess is a recurring motif in Southeast Asian folklore. It can be found in the origin myths of Cambodia, Annam, Laos, and Champa. Sometimes the stranger marries the *naga* king's daughter, and sometimes he marries a mortal princess.

All these stories seem to indicate a common basis in fact arising from Hindu explorations about the time of Christ. One theory suggests that the Hindus were not exploring, but were fleeing from the wrath of their king in India.

In any event, Hindu culture developed rapidly in Fu-nan. Within 200 years the savage tribe had been welded into a nation. By 300 A.D. Fu-nan was strong enough to conquer both Champa on the east coast and the Khmers of Chen-la in the central area of the Mekong plain.

The Chinese watched the development of this warlike nation. In order to establish a buffer state to prevent Fu-nan from reaching to the Chinese border, China invaded Annam in what is now North Vietnam. Once this buffer state was established, the Chinese made no further attempt to move south for another several hundred years.

The conquered Khmers of Chen-la absorbed Hindu culture from their Funanese masters and grew stronger while the Funanese themselves grew weaker. Internal struggles for the Funanese throne finally gave the Khmers an opportunity to strike for freedom. In 550 A.D., under their king, Kambu Svayambhuva, they overthrew the king of Fu-nan.

The jubilant Khmers enshrined Kambu as a folk hero and began to call themselves *Kambujadesa*—the sons of Kambu—instead of Khmers, a word whose true meaning has been lost. Eventually they dropped Chen-la as the name of their nation and it became Kambuja, which in turn became Cambodia in English.

The resulting empire lasted 250 years and then was destroyed by invading Malays. After the invaders were driven out, Kambuja made a dramatic comeback. In the Angkorean Age, beginning in the tenth century and extending to the beginning of the fifteenth century, the Khmers reached a marvelous peak of civilization and power at a time when Europe was sunk in the Dark Ages.

Then, suddenly, for reasons not clearly understood, this mighty empire collapsed. In a very short time it was forgotten. The decline was so great that when Europeans first penetrated the area in the mid-nineteenth century, they thought they had found a primeval people who had never advanced above savagery.

European explorers came into Indochina at this time as the vanguard for colonial expansion of their countries. The most famous of these was Henri Mouhot, a dedicated French naturalist. Passionately devoted to his profession, Mouhot fought his way through the jungles of Siam, Laos, and Cambodia for four years before dying of fever during his last expedition to Laos. His journal, published in Paris after his death, created a scientific sensation. Here, recorded for the first time, was scientific evidence that the supposedly primitive jungle of Cambodia once harbored a tremendous civilization undreamed of in Europe. The journal told how Mouhot left Saigon in January 1860, on a trip through central Cambodia. He stopped first at Oudong, about twenty miles up the Tonle Sap River from the present Cambodian capital at Phnom Penh. Here the explorer was received by the Second King. (It was then the curious custom in both Cambodia and Siam to have a substitute king. Knowledge of his exact duties has been obscured

The Khmers left ruins all over Cambodia. Many of their bridges are still in use.

in the mists of time, but he had absolutely no power and rarely was permitted to succeed the First King.)

This dignitary received Mouhot apparently on orders of the First King, Norodom, who was suspicious of all foreigners. A legend says that Norodom listened from behind a screen, but would not talk to the Frenchman himself. After questioning the scientist about his plans, the Khmers gave Mouhot permission to continue. He was supplied with both oxen and porters to carry his supplies.

Mouhot headed up the Tonle Sap River and then due north of the Great Lake. It was January and well past the rainy season, but the jungle was so thick the sun had not yet dried the wet ground. The wheels of the ox carts kept sinking into the mire. The porters sweated and strained as the party made slow progress. The trip was neither better nor worse than the others Mouhot had made in his nearly four years of explorations in Cochin China. Fever-bearing mosquitoes, blood-sucking leeches, hungry tigers, wild elephants, and poisonous snakes had become a part of his life. But there was one interesting difference about this trip. The further he penetrated into Cambodia, the more he heard of a mysterious city lost in the jungles ahead.

Mouhot kept a journal of the odd stories he had heard. One day, realizing it would be read later by other naturalists, he hastily added an apologetic note: "It seems a concession to ignorance that I should waste this much space to record a fable so lacking in originality of plot...."

As he penetrated deeper into the jungle the rumors became more persistent. "Lord, there is a city unlike anything man has ever dreamed of," an old Cambodian man told him at one village. "It is deep in the jungle where the angry gods hid it from man." Mouhot questioned the old man closely. Had he seen the city? He had not, but he knew it was true because the story came from his father who had heard it from his father. The lost city was a place of the dead. No person who valued his soul would dare go there.

Irritated, Mouhot wrote in his journal: "Stories of hidden cities in this part of the world grow more absurd as one gets deeper into the jungles." In his mind the lost city of Cambodia was in the same class with the fabled Atlantis, the Ophirian mines of King Solomon, and the lost continent of Mu.

Then, late one evening, the exploring party crossed a small river that fed into the mighty Mekong. As the porters prepared camp, Mouhot took advantage of the remaining daylight to gather new specimens for his collection. He had gone but a short distance when he saw a weird tower of stone. Trees had sprouted through cracks at the top, and giant gray roots, large as pythons, entwined it in a strangling embrace. Strange faces were carved on the stones.

Mouhot was stunned. As a scientist he recorded only fact and did not display his emotions. However, we can assume he felt as Pierre Lôti, the famous French writer, did later. Lôti wrote: "I looked at the tree-strangled towers that dwarfed me. Then all of a sudden my blood curdled as I saw an enormous smile looking down on me. . . ."

The tower was constructed of stone. This surprised Mouhot for he knew the nearest place the builders could have found sandstone was in the Dangrek Mountains, which were nearly fifty miles away on the Siamese border. The tower served no purpose as far as Mouhot could see.

By the scientist's reckoning, he was 300 miles northwest of Saigon and 200 miles east of Bangkok in Siam. He had encountered no Cambodian natives since leaving Tonle Lake 40 miles to the south. Then who had built this ancient tower and why? Why had it been located in such a remote spot? What did the strange faces mean? And why was such a marvel shunned by the natives?

As Mouhot was driven back by fading light, he stumbled on part of a giant face. It appeared as if blocks of stone had been set up and then carved to make the face. The eyes were missing. The snakelike tree roots had pushed the stone partially away, but the full stone mouth was intact. It was carved in a peculiar smile that was, in its own way, as mysterious as Leonardo da Vinci's Mona Lisa. In addition, the mysterious smile seemed to express a touch of pity as if the stone face felt sorry for those it looked down upon.

The Ta Prohn temple at Angkor Thom, left as it has been found, shows visitors how the entire city looked when Henri Mouhot discovered it between the trees.

A stone face of Lokesvara looks out from atop a gate to Angkor Thom.

The next day brought even more astonishing wonders. Mouhot found that he had discovered a true lost city and not just a monument, as he had originally thought. The strange tales he heard coming up the Tonle Sap River had been true after all.

Almost in total ruins, the city lay behind a wall pierced by a huge gate topped by four of the strange heads Mouhot had seen earlier. Outside the wall, and a short distance from the city, was a tremendous structure, much better preserved than the walled city. It lay inside a moat and was surrounded by a stone gallery that was half a mile square. A causeway wide enough for twenty people to walk abreast down it led across the moat to the entrance. The causeway was flanked by stone railings carved like great snakes, whose front ends reared up in the traditional form of the seven-headed *naga*— the cobra king.

Crossing the causeway, Mouhot found that the vast outer gallery surrounded a central building, which was a central tower flanked by four smaller towers. Familiar as he was with India, Mouhot recognized the shape as a replica in stone of Mount Meru, the Hindu heaven.

The gray stone looked very old. Yet the huge temple was remarkably well preserved. Mouhot could find no evidence that it had been occupied for centuries. Then why had the jungle not destroyed it as the snaking tree roots had destroyed the city beyond the wall? This was another mystery the French naturalist could not resolve.

One of the more astonishing things Mouhot found was the vast amount of carved stone. It appeared that no place had escaped the artists' chisels. The outer galleries alone had over two miles of bas relief that appeared to Mouhot to be part of the *Ramayana,* the classic Indian tale of Prince Rama and his friend, Hanuman, the white king of the monkeys. In other places on the outer wall the carving consisted of intricate designs, some so delicate and so elaborate that it had the appearance of stone lace. Mouhot marveled as he thought of the years of labor that had gone into constructing and decorating this vast wonder.

One of the odder aspects of the temple was the enormous num-

Of the thousands of apsaras, *or heavenly dancers, carved on the walls of Angkor Wat and Angkor Thom, no two are exactly alike.*

ber of *apsaras,* or heavenly dancing girls, carved on the walls. There seemed to be thousands of them and no two appeared to be exactly alike.

Later Mouhot spent considerable time in the ruined city. It appeared not to have been destroyed by men, but by giant tree roots that pried the stones apart. Even though everything was in ruins, Mouhot could see that the rocks were as elaborately carved as were those of the temple outside the walls. In one pile he found hundreds of pieces of eyes and mouths, indicating that there had been a clustering of the curious four-faced towers like the one that topped the gate to the city.

Again, like the temple, there was no sign of human life or any real evidence that people had ever been there. He saw plenty of jungle life. Inquisitive gibbons swung and chattered in the trees. Birds flushed at his approach. Huge butterflies fluttered about and the deadly cobra, its hood spread, slithered across the fallen stones as he approached.

What Mouhot discovered that day in January 1860 was the lost city of Angkor Thom (*Angkor* meaning city and *Thom* meaning great).

As he climbed over the rocks, Henri Mouhot asked himself: "What manner of people built all this? Where did they come from? Where did they go and why did they leave? Why did they use stone in a land where even kings live in wooden palaces? Why was so vast a city built in this uninhabited spot?"

Mouhot delayed his trip north for two weeks while he explored the ruins. He left with deep regret, knowing that he had not fully uncovered all that was hidden by the heavy jungle growth. He summed up what he had seen by writing in his journal: "This is greater than anything left to us by Greece and Rome!"

CHAPTER 3

****

THE RISE
OF ANGKOR THOM

IN HIS TRAVELS northward Henri Mouhot now paid eager attention
to native tales of the lost city, but he found little that would account
for the mysterious stone ruins. The true story had dissolved into
legend and myth.

One old man told him that giants appeared and built it in a
single day. Another story claimed the city was built by a mighty
warrior who offended the gods who then made him a leper. The
misfortunes of the leper king were visited upon his people. Tragedy followed tragedy until the city crumbled in ruins.

About five years after Mouhot, the redoubtable Anna Leonowens rode an elephant 200 miles from Bangkok to see the ruins.
Anna is the lady famous in our time as the heroine of *Anna and*

the King of Siam. In an age when women stayed at home she not only went to Bangkok to teach the prince, but later became a war correspondent. She thought nothing of striking out through 200 miles of jungle dangers on an elephant to see some strange ruins.

After her return she wrote of marveling "at the work of a race of whose existence the Western nations know nothing, who have no name in history, yet who builded in a style surpassing the best works of the modern world—stupendous, beautiful, enduring."

King Mongkut of Siam gave her a Sanskrit manuscript of a Siamese version recounting the building of Angkor Thom. It must be remembered that Siam had several times conquered Angkor and ruled the area, at which time the Siamese were trying to claim the Cambodian provinces that included Angkor, and they naturally gave a Siamese identity to the prince in the story. The age of the manuscript was not given by Mrs. Leonowens, but it certainly was written a long time before Mouhot discovered the lost city.

According to the story, the beautiful princess Thawadee had a son by the supreme god Indra who lived on Mount Meru, the sacred mountain. The king, Thawadee's father, did not know that Prince Somannass was the child of the god, and he banished both the prince and his mother. The poor girl wandered through the forest until Phra (lord) Indra saw what had happened. He came down to earth and took the form of a Brahman (priest) to protect Princess Thawadee and his son, Prince Somannass.

Indra made them a home in a mountain cave where the boy grew to manhood. The manuscript tells us that he was a youth of "wonderous beauty. The melody of his voice tamed the wild creatures of the forest, and charmed even the seven-headed dragons." Now Indra, who had returned to Mount Meru, started to yearn for his son. In a flash of lightning he took the boy into the heavens to live.

"Here," Anna Leonowens tells us, "he was initiated in all the mysteries of life and death, with all wisdom and foresight. His celestial royal father showed him the stars coursing hither and thither on their errands of love and mercy; showed him comets with tails of fire flashing through the centuries, spreading confusion and havoc. He heard the music of the spheres, he tasted heavenly food and drank of the river that flows from the Most Highest." (From *An English Governess at the Siamese Court*, by Anna Leonowens, published in 1870.)

The young man was not happy in heaven and asked Indra to permit him to return to earth. Reluctantly, Indra agreed but insisted that his son must live in a heaven on earth. He sent a host of angels down to Kambuja to build a home fit for the son of heaven. They built it in a single night, as the Cambodian legend has it. Phya Naghk (Naga) helped the builders by showing them places where gold and stone could be found. In gratitude they placed stone images of the snake king in the city. Finally, as a tribute to Princess Thawadee the builders carved thousands of dancing girls on the walls.

At first scientific investigators could not find any better explanation for the origin of the lost city. They called the Khmers a vanished race, for they were sure the primitive Cambodians could not have descended from men who could build such a marvel. However, time has proven them wrong. French archeologist Georges Coedés worked for years comparing photographs of modern Cambodians with faces carved on the walls of Angkor Thom. His work clearly shows that today's Cambodian is a true son of Kambu.

Solution of this mystery resulted in another: How and why did so great a civilization sink so quickly into near savagery? Why did the Angkoreans abandon such a great city? And why were the people forever after afraid to return?

The answers have come slowly from the work of l'Ecole française d'extrème Orient, a school founded in Hanoi by the French to study Indochinese history, with a branch devoted to Angkor alone. For more than half a century now, men of the French School of the Far East have fought the jungle to restore a number of the Angkorean ruins. At the same time, they have slowly unraveled some of the mystery of the Khmer past. Old Chinese documents, bits of history from Siam and Java, wall inscriptions at Angkor, and stele have all added fragments to the story. But, with it all, it remains a story with many long gaps.

Chen-la revolted against Fu-nan in 550 A.D., and the resulting empire of Chen-la lasted 200 years. After the death of King Jay-avarman around 750 A.D., a power struggle split the empire into Upper Chen-la and Lower Chen-la. Lower Chen-la included the present Vietnam Mekong delta area and went as far north as Phnom Penh. Nothing is known of the next thirty years, but in 780 A.D. the curtain of mystery lifts slightly. A manuscript written by an Arabian traveler of Java tells a curious story of Chen-la's fall. A "traveler's tale" has long been an expression for exaggerated stories, and it may well be that this traveler was also enlarging upon the truth. However, it is the only written word we have of Chen-la during this period. As a result Cambodian historians include the tale.

This much is history: About 780 A.D. a powerful family called the Sailendra, or Lords of the Mountain, built an empire that included Sumatra, Java, and much of Malaya. They did not invade Southeast Asia, but made frequent pirate raids on its coastal cities.

So much for history. Now for the traveler's tale: The Arabian manuscript claims that Lower Chen-la had a boastful young king. His name was not given, but historians believe it was Mahipati-varman. The king was discussing the Sailendra raids with his grand vizier when he suddenly became violent with rage. Nothing would give him greater pleasure, he said, than to receive the head of the Lord of the Mountain on a golden platter. The minister was alarmed, as Sulayman the Arab traveler relates. He knew the power and pride of the Sailendra ruler. He begged the young king to stop making such statements.

The angry king repeated his wish, and in time spies reported them to the Sailendra in his palace in Sumatra. The Lord of the Mountain immediately assembled a fleet of war galleys. Announcing that he was going to inspect his kingdom, he crossed the South China Sea instead and sailed up the Mekong. He captured the surprised Khmer capital without a fight. Seating himself on the throne of the Khmers, he had the captive Mahipativarman dragged before him. "Had you wished for my kingdom," he told the captive, "I would take yours. Had you wished for my wealth, I would steal yours. Instead, you wished for my head, and that is what I will take of yours."

He had Mahipativarman beheaded. Then, after ordering the prime minister to select a new king of the Khmers, the Sailendra sailed back to Sumatra with the head. According to Sulayman's account, he took nothing else from the kingdom he conquered and would not permit any of his men to take any loot. When he got home the king displayed the Khmer's head on a golden platter while he related to his court what he had done. Then he had the head preserved in clear wine and sent it to the new king of the Khmers with a letter in which he wrote that he took no glory in his act, but had done it solely to protect his reputation before the world. He succeeded in this for Sulayman tells us: "When this reached the ears of the kings of India and China, the Maharaja of Zabag—the Sailendra—rose in their estimation. And the new king of the Khmers turned his face in the direction of the Maharaja's land of Zabag every morning and bowed his head to the ground in homage." This anecdote is an indication that Sailendra kept Cambodia in subjugation for a number of years. Nothing actually is certain about the next twenty years.

Then in 800 A.D. the Lord of the Mountain sent a young man from Sumatra to be king of the Khmers. He, too, is one of the unexplained mysteries of Cambodia's past. There are two conflicting stories about his origin. One claims he was a prince of the Khmer dynasty who was taken back to Sumatra while a child to be trained to be a puppet king for the Sailendra. The other story says he was remotely related to the ruling dynasty of the Khmers and had no direct claim to the throne except the power of the Sailendra.

The inscriptions on the temples raised during his sixty-year reign are politely quiet about the king's origin. One inscribed stone that dates from this period makes this odd reference: "A great lotus which no longer has a stalk, he rose like a new flower," which has been interpreted to mean that Kambuja had no king and he came as a new blossom. While he actually became king in 802, some accounts claim that he came to Kambuja twelve years earlier. The years between his arrival and his coronation were spent in bitter fighting to unite Upper and Lower Chen-la. When he took the crown he also took the name of Jayavarman II, greatest of the Chen-la kings.

The new king reunited Upper Chen-la and Lower Chen-la. At the same time he fought off an invasion from Champa, which gave him an acceptable excuse for building up a strong army without arousing the suspicion of his Sailendra master in Java.

As his strength grew, Jayavarman built a new capital city on Phnom Kulen, a mountain not far from the later site of Angkor Thom. Here he felt sufficiently secure from foreign invasion to declare his independence from the Sailendra. The King of the Mountain learned, as the French would 1,100 years later, that a Khmer king is a poor subject to use as a puppet.

At the same time, Jayavarman took another drastic step which would profoundly affect the Khmers. He introduced the cult of the *devaraja*, or god-king, with the cooperation of a Brahman named Mahendraparvata, a priest "learned in the ways of magic," as old inscriptions tell us. For a long time it was assumed that this great priest came from India, but now some scholars believe he was a Khmer who studied under priests in India. He evidently had a tremendous reputation among the Khmers when Jayavarman brought him to Phnom Kulen.

The theory that Jayavarman and the priest evolved was that the Khmer king was part of god himself. After his death on earth the king would reunite with his greater god self. Being a god, the king was therefore greater than all other kings in the world. He demanded not only the obedience and respect due a king, but also the reverence and worship due a god.

Jayavarman picked Siva, third of the Hindu trinity with Brahma and Vishnu, as his sacred self. Siva was considered both the giver

and taker of life—the lord of birth and death. He was often represented, especially in Khmer temple art, in the form of a stone
image of the male sexual organ, which was known as a *lingam.*

Successive kings continued the cult of the king-god, but had
the right to choose the god with which they wished to be identified. The later builder of Angkor Wat, for example, saw himself
as the earthly body of Vishnu, the preserver of life. It is not
known why Jayavarman picked Siva. It could have been because
this god, in the form of the lingam, had been worshipped in Southeast Asia since the introduction of Hindu culture into Fu-nam
600 years before. Thus, there were no radical changes in the
religion to disturb priests and worshippers. Jayavarman merely
built his god cult upon the firm foundation of a popular religious
belief of his time. He simply stated that he was Siva on earth. He
pointed out that he had used his divine power to give his people
independence from the Sailendra and promised to lead them to still
greater glory.

It was more than only megalomania that made Jayavarman pro-
claim himself a god on earth. This religious act united the country
and made possible the development and immortality of the empire that followed, because the weird and wonderful structures
Henri Mouhot described do not really represent the city of Angkor
Thom, but only its religious temples.

Under the *devaraja* system each succeeding king felt obligated
to build himself a funerary temple in which his spirit could reside
after death. Apparently none of them wished to be reunited with
his sacred greater self on Mount Meru. Instead they built stone
replicas of the sacred mountain on earth where their spirits could
live for all eternity. It was these stone temples that defied the
jungle rot while the wooden structures of the city vanished. The
stones preserved almost all we know of the vanished empire of
the Khmers.

****

CHAPTER 4

THE GREAT KING

IN TIME JAYAVARMAN II became so powerful that lesser kings were afraid to attack Cambodia. He was then able to move his capital from the mountain to the lowland. Here, where there was ample fish and rice, Jayavarman built a new capital, Hariharalaya, which soon had a population of a million people.

The king died in 850 A.D., leaving a powerful nation. Kings succeeded kings. The two who followed Jayavarman II were successful in preserving Kambuja's power. The third king, Yasovarman I, wanted a capital with his own name. He moved the seat of government to the site of present-day Angkor Thom and built Yasodharapura.

Then trouble developed. With the death of the second of the

The approach to Angkor Wat, greatest of the old Khmer ruins.

two succeeding kings, Yasanavarman II, the king's brother deposed the dead monarch's eldest son and crowned himself as Jayavarman IV. The deposed son and his younger brother led a revolt to unseat the usurper. They captured the capital, but were unable to defeat their uncle's forces entirely. Jayavarman IV set up a new capital. Once again Cambodia was divided, with Jayavarman ruling the southern half and the two brothers ruling the northern section.

Curiously, the two brothers reigned in Yasodharapura as dual monarchs and dual *devarajas,* or god-kings. Each had his own throne, court, and *purohitas,* or royal bishops. Although they maintained separate royal etiquette, they worked as one in trying to defeat their uncle toward reunification of the two kingdoms.

The conflict continued until the brothers died. Since they were younger than their uncle, Jayavarman IV, but died first, it is presumed that they were assassinated.

When the brothers died, Jayavarman IV was able to extend his rule over all Cambodia. He continued, however, to rule from his own capital Chok Gargyar. The seat of government was not brought back to Yasodharapura until about 950 A.D., where it remained for the next 227 years. During these two centuries, the Khmer nation rose to the peak of its glory.

The man responsible for Cambodia's golden age called himself Suryavarman I. He was not a Cambodian by birth, although he may have been one by blood. He was first ruler of a tiny Malay kingdom. Then, about 997 A.D., he landed a Malay military force in the Mekong delta. He called the reigning king of Cambodia, Jayavarman V, a usurper and claimed the throne himself through the blood lines of his mother, who was a Cambodian princess. He fought for nine years through the reigns of three kings before conquering the country and making himself king.

Once firmly in power, Suryavarman introduced Buddhism as the state religion, but permitted the cults of Siva and Vishnu to continue. Religion at this time was confused. The king was installed in the different temples as the king-god of the Sivaites and the

Vishnuites, and at the same time he was worshipped in the Buddhist temples as the reincarnation on earth of the spirit of Buddha.

A wall inscription at Angkor Thom provides an insight into the character of this forceful man. He forced 4,000 officials to swear to this oath: "If there be war, we pledge to fight faithfully for the king's cause without thinking of our own lives . . . as our lives are dedicated to the king's service to the day of our death. . . . If we do not stick to this oath of allegiance to the great king—may he reign in glory through the ages—we ask that he inflict punishment upon us. If we hide to escape carrying out this oath, may we be reborn in the thirty-two hells as long as there is a sun and moon."

The king put such fear into his officials that his reign was free from the court intrigue that ruined so many previous monarchs. But this peace lasted only his lifetime. When he died trouble started again. The new king tried to banish Buddhism and faced an angry revolt. The king of Champa took advantage of the Khmer religious trouble to invade Cambodia.

For a while it appeared that Cambodia would be destroyed as a nation, as Fu-nan had been before. An inscription from this period tells how a large part of the Cambodian army revolted. When it began to appear that the struggle was lost, the Khmer hero Sangrama rallied loyalist forces, put down the revolt, and defeated the Chams. But Sangrama did not feel that his work was appreciated. He withdrew in embittered exile while the king's favor fell on less able men. While Sangrama sulked, the Chams regrouped and launched a new attack. Sangrama came out of exile to again save his country. He could not, however, reunite the divided Cambodian forces, and the division continued for ninety more years. Finally, in 1113 a new king, Suryavarman II, restored unity and began a series of plundering wars. He attacked the Annamites in present North Vietnam, hit the Chams to the east, and then turned on the Mon tribes to the west.

The treasure and slaves he seized from these conquests were used to build himself a funerary temple. He conceived of it as the greatest monument the world had ever known. He came close to achieving his ideal, for the monument is Angkor Wat, the supreme achievement of Khmer art and one of the true wonders of the world. No written account has yet given an adequate description of the temple. Photographs do not tell the full story either; although they show the details perfectly, they fail to capture the immensity and elaborate design that stun the eye when Angkor Wat is beheld in its natural glory.

Here are comments from some people who have seen it:

"It is greater than anything left to us by Greece and Rome." Henri Mouhot.

"Worthy of being ranked with the best in the world." Georges Grosier, French archeologist.

"I was haunted by the pyramids of Egypt until I saw Angkor." James Michener, American novelist.

"If nothing else remained of all their works, Angkor Wat would be enough to mark the Khmers as one of the great races that time has produced." Robert J. Casey, American journalist.

"It is the Asian contemporary of Notre Dame de Paris and Chartres Cathedral in France and of Ely and Lincoln Cathedrals in England. But in spaciousness and splendor it is more ambitious than any of these." Malcolm MacDonald, British diplomat.

"The majestic ruins of the watt [sic] stand like a petrified dream of some Michelangelo of the giants—more impressive in its loneliness, more elegant in its grace, than aught that Greece and Rome have left us." Anna Leonowens. Later she added: "We reluctantly departed, feeling that the world contains no monument more impressive, more inspiring than, in its desolation and yet wondrous preservation, the temple of Maha Naghkon [Angkor] Watt."

"Suddenly there looms into view the five central towers of Angkor Wat. The temples of Karnak, the ruins of ancient Greece, the stateliest piles of medieval Europe have paled into insignificance. Spellbound, I watched the sun . . . reveal the immensity of a masterpiece the jungle hid for more than 300 years." Leigh Williams, British author who spent twenty years working teak in Siam.

Although these opinions may sound extravagant, Angkor Wat is as impressive a man-made sight as will be found on this earth. A statistical description is insufficient.

Angkor Wat is a stone replica of Mount Meru, the Hindu home of the gods. It was built in rising terraces, each depicting a level of society and terminating in the holiest of holies where the god dwelled in a central tower.

The temple was dedicated to Vishnu, the preserver, with whom Suryavarman identified himself. It was intended to be the king's tomb after death. The meaning behind this was different from the Egyptian custom of entombing their kings in pyramids. The Egyptians sought to preserve the body of their kings, to insure their immortality in a future world. The Khmers, on the other hand, burned their dead. If anything mortal of the king was placed in the great funerary temple, it would have been his ashes, to represent his "essence" or the concentration of all his physical powers. This might be termed his "soul," but to the Khmers it meant more than Westerners mean by the same word.

The huge structure is surrounded by a moat that represents the cosmic ocean that surrounds the earth. Crossing the moat is a causeway with naga-motif balustrades. It leads to a stone gallery that forms a square about the central mass of the temple. To get to the central structure one must pass through cloistered courtyards where every wall is embroidered with stone carvings. After climbing three levels to the central sanctuary, one reaches a gallery that connects the four corner towers that hem in the main tower.

These towers, or *prasats,* represent the lotus blossom ready to burst into bloom. The central tower is 215 feet high, and the circumference of the gallery is a half mile. From the carved stone windows of the upper gallery, one can look down on the maze of cloisters and courtyards, as well as out over the thick jungle that surrounds the ruins.

Most of the movable treasures have been taken to the national museum in Phnom Penh, but occasionally one stumbles on a piece of remaining statuary. The strangely smiling faces festooned with cobwebs evoke a weird atmosphere in the dark galleries.

One of the first questions the viewer asks is, how was it built? But there is no clue to the answer. The enormity of its mass may have fostered the legend that it was the work of a heavenly host. The huge stone blocks had to have been brought from a quarry that was two days' journey away, then they had to be cut, dressed, and fitted. Some are so huge that modern engineers do not see how they could have been lifted into the upper galleries with the primitive means at the Khmers' disposal. The miles of bas reliefs on the outer galleries seem to be the work of centuries of carving. One modern engineer has estimated that it would have taken 300 years to complete Angkor Wat. Yet we know that it was completed in about fifty years.

Many writers have assumed that the temple was built by slaves captured in Suryavarman's wars. They depict straining, sweating men staggering under harness, spurred by whips of brutal masters, pulling blocks of stone over jungle roads. However, there is no proof of this or anything else regarding the building of the temple. But one thing is certain: no king—regardless of his might—can capture enough artists to carve in stone the miles of highly artistic work found on the walls of Angkor Wat. Where were so many stone carvers found? This is another of the unexplained mysteries of the Khmers.

By the time of Suryavarman, the Annamites in what is now North Vietnam had won their independence from China. After Annam became strong enough to be a threat to its southern neighbors, Suryavarman joined with Champa in attacks on the Annamite nation. Chinese records show that he first sent an ambassador to China to assure this powerful country that the attack was not unfriendly to it. Annam successfully withstood the attack and later made peace with Champa. Suryavarman, smarting under the defeat, made plans for a new attack. The king of Champa refused to join in the new war on Annam. Suryavarman flew into a rage and invaded Champa instead. He killed the king of Champa and sacked the capital, Vijaya, in 1144.

When Suryavarman died in about 1150, it was supposed that he would be succeeded by his son Jayavarman. Instead the young man was shoved aside by a relative who took the name of Dharanindravarman II. He reigned for ten years and was succeeded by Yasovarman II.

During this decade, Jayavarman made no attempt to claim the throne himself. One of the most remarkable of the old Khmers, he was a devout Buddhist, and in keeping with Buddhist beliefs he refused to fight for what was his. It is also possible that he did not then want to be king. The state religion had reverted to Sivaism, and, if he became king, Jayavarman would be conscience-bound to restore Buddhism. He remembered only too well how attempts to change religions in the past had exposed Cambodia to its foreign enemies. So instead of causing more trouble, Jayavarman went into exile in Champa.

When Yasovarman died in 1165, Jayavarman came back, expecting to be crowned at last. Instead, the throne was seized by a rebel chief, Tribhuvanadityavarman—he of the longest and most unpronounceable name in Khmer history. Jayavarman, finding the new king firmly in control, again refused to fight for his birthright and went back into exile. Tribhuvanadityavarman reigned from 1165 to about 1177. Then carelessness and an arrogant belief in his power brought Cambodia to the worst crisis in its history.

The king's policies caused a series of revolts. They were unsuccessful, but the king of Champa took advantage of the internal disorders to invade Cambodia. The Cham army was driven back in savage jungle fighting. Tribhuvanadityavarman thought it would take the Chams another twenty years to rebuild their shattered army, but the Chams got an able Chinese army commander to reorganize their military machine, which he quickly did, and Champa again attacked Cambodia.

Acting on the Chinese officer's advice, the Chams did not attack through the jungle frontier as before. They amassed a fleet of galleys and came up the Mekong River. The major part of the Khmer army was on the northeast frontier guarding against an expected attack by the Annamite army. The Chams sailed into Tonle Sap before the Khmers knew they were coming. Then it was only a forty-mile hike over good roads from the Great Lake to Yasodharapura. The Khmers could not pull their army back from the Annam border quickly enough, and the Chams easily swept over the wooden palisades guarding the city. The defenders of Yasodharapura were slaughtered, the city sacked and burned, and the king assassinated. The victors did not try to hold the city. They piled the loot into their galleys and returned to Champa by sea.

This attack occurred in 1177 A.D. With the king dead, Cambodia was plunged into total anarchy. No claimant to the throne could muster sufficient political strength to bring order out of the chaos. The situation was worse than at the time of the Sailendra conquest, where there had been a strong central government to maintain internal order. Now there was only the law of the sword and the spear.

The Chams made plans to take over the whole country and annex it to Champa. Cambodia was in such a state of anarchy and disorder that the people could not organize any defense except an organization of small guerrilla bands who kept harassing the Cham army. Fighting raged from one end of Cambodia to the other. The people feared total destruction.

****

CHAPTER 5

JAYAVARMAN VII, HERO OF HEROES

IN ONE OF those curious reversals of character that happen often in fiction but seldom in real life, it was the man who previously would not fight who saved Cambodia from total ruin.

Jayavarman grew old while he watched the devastation of his country. Finally, the ruinous attacks of the Chams and the anarchy in Cambodia made the peace-loving prince realize that the sword was his country's only salvation in these troubled times. Therefore, in 1181, when he was fifty years old, Jayavarman turned away from his peaceful beliefs. Moving swiftly and decisively, he united the warring Khmer factions. Then, while he still had the advantage of surprise, he rallied a fighting force and hit the invading Cham army just outside the ruins of Yasodharapura which the Chams had burned.

He achieved a surprising victory which put heart back into the Khmers. The nation rallied behind the new hero in a desperate attempt to save their nation. He continued to win battles, but the decisive victory was a naval engagement on Tonle Lake. Details of the fighting were later carved onto the walls of a temple in the new capital Jayavarman built. They show boats ramming into each other while closely packed warriors hurl spears. In the water, swimmers brave crocodiles to make daring amphibious attacks on rival craft.

When the Chams were finally defeated, Jayavarman smashed Champa. Then by conquest he carved out an empire stretching into Malaya, present-day Thailand, and possibly into sections of Burma. Under him, the Khmer nation reached its greatest expansion and ruled over almost all of Southeast Asia.

The king built with feverish activity. His greatest achievement was rebuilding the burned capital, which was now called Angkor Thom—the Great City—the name by which we know it today. Angkor was circled with a moat, and a stone wall took the place of the wooden palisades burned by the Chams. The wall was pierced by four gates topped by the four faces that startled Henri Mouhot. The king also built irrigation canals and water reservoirs and raised the highways to prevent flooding when the Tonle Sap spread out in the rainy season.

Hundreds of new temples were built, including the mysterious Bayon. The reason for building the curious Bayon has never been determined. There is nothing like it anywhere on earth. As an artistic work it is hardly in a class with Angkor Wat, the Egyptian temples of Karnak, the ruins of Greece and Rome, or even the Gothic cathedrals of Europe. Its main claim to fame lies in its inscrutability and awesomeness.

The Bayon sits on a raised stone terrace. From a distance, it looks like a rocky crag. But as one approaches, there appear to be upjutting rocks that are in reality closely packed towers grouped around a central spire. These towers are somewhat like the *prasats* —lotus blossom towers—so familiar in Angkor Wat. But here each

The four-faced images of Jayavarman VII look down from hundreds of towers in Angkor Thom, in the strange pavillion known as the Bayon.

Closeup shows one of the four faces of Lokesvara in the Bayon. Archeologists believe that stone carvers used Jayavarman's features for their model.

Partial restoration of one of the Bayon towers. The massive blocks were piled on top of each other without mortar.

is studded with four faces staring out with curious smiles in each of the four cardinal directions. The towers vary in height; some are so low that the stone faces stare straight into the visitors' eyes. Walking along the twisted path between them is like walking through a labyrinth.

In 1912 Jean Commaille of the French School of the Far East began cutting away the jungle growth from the ruins of the Bayon. Piece by piece he reassembled the fallen stones and restored the strange monument. Since that time the Angkor ruins have been under constant study by the school's archeologists, who should be the supreme authorities. But unfortunately they do not always agree with each other. To further complicate matters, writers and students periodically advance more theories.

There are 50 towers and 200 of the great stone faces in the Bayon. It is an unnerving experience to walk along the upper terrace, for no matter in which direction you turn, you face the stone eyes. One can agree with Pierre Lôti, who stated: "My blood curdled . . . I was being observed from all sides."

Henri Parmentier, who spent most of his adult life reconstructing the Angkor ruins, called the Bayon "profoundly affecting and romantic. The visitor is oppressed by an evil sensation."

Henri Marshal, curator of the Angkor group, wrote in his *Archeological Guide to the Temples of Angkor*: "Particularly by moonlight, one feels as if he were visiting a temple in another world. . . . One can imagine one has returned to a fabulous era of legends, when the god Indra built a temple for his son's marriage to the daughter of the king of the *nagas*."

The stone faces were originally identified as "the four faces of Siva." (In fact, Robert J. Casey wrote a book about Angkor with that title in 1929.) Then in the early 1930s archeologists of the French School of the Far East made discoveries indicating that the four-face motif was Buddhist rather than Sivaic. In this theory the four-faced images are the Bodhisattva Avalokitesvara. In Mahayana Buddhism, the Bodhisattva is a person who has attained the state of enlightment necessary to be a Buddha. Instead of passing

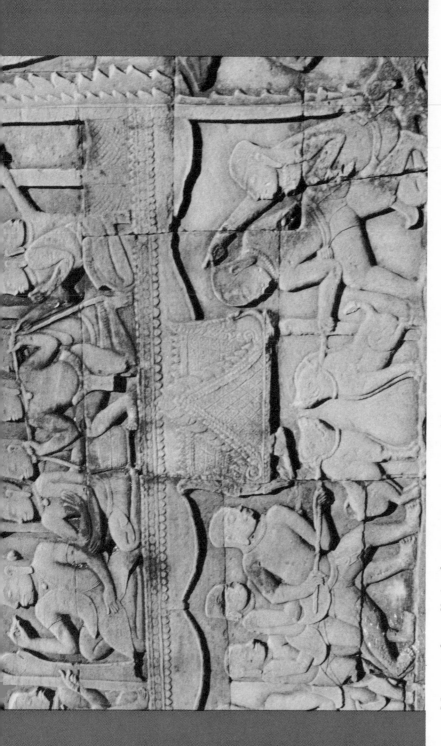

Many of the walls in the Bayon are carved with genre or everyday scenes of Angkorean life. This one shows a wild boar fight. Trainers hold the animals on leashes. The figure with the upraised arm is a referee.

into Nirvana, he elects to stay on earth to help the less fortunate. In his curious smile, the Bodhisattva—called *Lokesvara* in Cambodia—is expressing his pity for mankind's plight, a theory which supposes that Jayavarman VII saw himself as Lokesvara, a Buddha on earth. The faces are supposedly the king's portraits in his god-king role.

The Indian historian, Manomohan Ghosh, in *A History of Cambodia,* published in Saigon in 1960, argues against the French claim that the faces are of Lokesvara. He insists that they are Siva and that the school's authorities are also wrong in attributing the Bayon to the time of Jayavarman VII. Ghosh dates it back to Yasovarman who built the first city on the site of Angkor. The secret of the Bayon has not yet been explained to everyone's satisfaction.

There are two other oddities about the Bayon: It is the only Khmer temple not surrounded by its own wall, and it is the only temple whose carvings depict the life of everyday people.

What Jayavarman had in mind when he assembled this jungle of stone faces has never been determined. There is almost the impression that the Bayon served as a junkyard or attic where the excess that would not fit elsewhere in Angkor was put. However, the temple is in the exact center of the city. It is inconceivable that a temple erected in this paramount position could have been anything haphazard. It must have been carefully planned and built in this odd manner for a definite reason.

There are two clues that might give a possible reason for the temple's existence: the absence of a temple wall, and the depictions of ordinary people going about their work. These clues indicate that the temple was open to the general public. The other so-called temples were not; they were tombs of dead kings whose spirits lived on in their imitation heavens.

The four-faced towers were possibly intended to completely awe the common people who came to worship in the Bayon. Everywhere they looked they could see the eyes of the god-king upon them. At the same time the worshippers would be impressed

by the king's love for them, shown in the bas reliefs of them at
work and play. There are also many detailed carvings showing
the king driving out the Chams, which were to remind them that
the nation owed its life to the king's might. And if the modern
visitor is awed by the labyrinth of faces, what must have been its
effect on superstitious natives? Surely it filled them with fear,
awe, and a firm belief in the omnipotence of the Buddha-raja who
gave up paradise to remain on earth for their benefit.

Jayavarman was also famous for building hospitals. An inscription has been found claiming that "he felt the afflictions of his
subjects more than his own, because the suffering of the people
constitute the suffering of the king, more than his own suffering."
This passage has been quoted many times by writers in an attempt to connect this greatest of old Khmer kings with the curious
legend of the Leper King.

On a terrace near the Bayon in Angkor Thom there is a nude
statute of a seated man. It is the only unclothed statute in the city.
According to legend it represents the Leper King who once ruled
Angkor. French scientists deny that the statute represents a leper,
but do not deny that the Khmers once had a king afflicted with
this disease. Also, Chinese records claim Angkor was founded by
a leper, and there is an Indian report that a Kambujan monarch
once traveled to India for treatment for leprosy.

The Cambodian legend of the Leper King does not name the
monarch, but the outline of the story certainly implicates Jayavarman VII. Robert J. Casey obtained the following story from native
sources in 1929. There was once a mighty king who drove out
invaders to save his country from ruin. Just before the last crucial
battle he was told by a soothsayer that he would win, but that he
would face great adversity at the same time. The fortune teller
added cryptically that the king would also find two precious jewels
in the mud.

The king fought his battle and won. As he was riding in tri-
umph back to Angkor, an old woman ran from the cheering
crowd. She threw her arms about the king and kissed him. Only

then did the horrified people realize that she was a leper, and the king caught the incurable disease from her. (In those days it was believed that a leper passed the disease to all he touched.) The Royal Council shut the leper king in an isolated chapel for the protection of the court. Food and water were shoved in to him, but none would approach the unfortunate man.

In the palace there were 4,000 dancing girls like the ones carved on Angkor's walls today. Two of them felt sorry for the king, shut away in his prison. Though it was forbidden for anyone to approach the monarch, the two girls worked secretly in the night and dug a tunnel that led to him, and they served him faithfully for the rest of his life. It is said that the king burst into tears when he realized that the fortune teller's prophecy had come true. In the mire of his despair he found two living jewels.

Whether or not one of their kings was really a leper is a trivial matter in the history of a people, but the idea has seized the public imagination. The statue is one of the main stops on the guided tour of Angkor and the Terrace of the Leper King is marked on the maps. The story of the king and his living jewels is a favorite of the guides.

Leper or not, Jayavarman was never imprisoned. He was fifty years old when he assumed the throne of the Khmers, and he ruled for thirty-four years. During his full life he saved his country from invaders, rebuilt its capital, raised Kambuja to the peak of its might and glory, and did more for the common people than any monarch had ever done before him. He was the greatest of the Khmer kings.

The last years of Jayavarman VII's life coincided with the conquest of China by the Mongol emperor Genghis Khan. The Mongols, occupied with putting down Chinese revolts, had no time for Southeast Asia during the reigns of the two kings who followed Jayavarman VII. After that the situation changed, and in 1259, Kublai Khan, grandson of Genghis, began attacks in the south. His pressure on North Vietnam drove out the Annamites, who migrated southward to eventually destroy Champa so they could take its land. Kublai Khan also launched attacks on the Thai tribes occupying China's Yunnan province. The Thais refused to submit to the Mongols. They migrated southward into the Mon territory, overcoming the weaker natives there and settling in what is now Thailand (Siam).

Neither of these racial migrations affected the Khmers at the time, but would have profound effect later. The locations of the Annamites in what had been Champa and the Thais in the Mon territory put Cambodia directly between two nations of ferocious fighters, the Annamites and the Thais. In time this would lead to the destruction of the Khmer nation and turn Angkor Thom into a ghost city.

While these changes were going on, Angkor was ruled by Jayavarman VIII (1243–1295). Little is known of this man except that he disgraced a famous name by being a coward. He huddled in his palace, afraid to leave for fear of assassination. When he died in 1295, his son-in-law killed the lawful successor. The murderer then became king when his wife—the dead king's daughter—stole the Prah Kahn, the sacred sword of authority supposedly given to the first king of Angkor by the god Indra. With the "lightning of Indra" in his hand, the usurper automatically became king under the name Indravarman III. In the same year that Indravarman stole the throne, Kublai Khan died in China. His successor and grandson, Timur Khan, sent a combined trade and diplomatic mission to Angkor. In the group was a highly observant ambassador named Chou Ta-kuan.

Chou spent a year in Angkor Thom between 1296 and 1297. He kept a journal of what he saw, and in later years, when the memory of the Khmers had been forgotten, Chou's story was discovered and translated. It was dismissed as fiction, for no one believed that such a marvelous city could have existed in the Indochina jungles.

After Henri Mouhot electrified Europe with his vivid account of the ruins of Angkor, there was a rush to re-examine old documents for clues to the mystery of the lost city. In addition to

Chou's journal, investigators found Sulayman's account of the fall of Chen-la and also a reference to Angkor in an old Portuguese manuscript. Chou's account was the best of all; it has proven an historical gold mine, for he has not yet made a single mistake. The buildings he mentioned have been identified; his account of city life is verified to a large extent by the genre carvings on the Bayon walls; inscriptions and stele further bear out the Chinese ambassador's accuracy.

Chou's manuscript was first translated in 1800 by Abel Rémusat, a French authority on China. In 1902 Paul Pelliot made a new translation for publication in the bulletin of the French School of the Far East. When Pelliot died in 1940, a revised French translation was found among his effects; it was published in Paris in 1952. The manuscript has never been fully translated into English. However, many travel writers, including Somerset Maugham and Robert J. Casey, translated excerpts from the French version for use in their own accounts of Angkor.

Chou was a lively commentator. Little escaped his inquisitive eye. He recorded everything from history to gossip. The result is a vivid picture of life in Angkor Thom when the Khmer capital was one of the great cities of the world.

CHAPTER 6

LIFE IN ANGKOR THOM

ONE THING CHOU approved of in Angkor was the respect paid to the king. "These people know how a prince should be treated," he wrote after watching a royal parade crossing the plaza in front of the Terrace of the Elephants in the central part of the city. In Chou's time the wooden palace and homes of the court dignitaries covered the terrace and the area behind it. The use of gold leaf made the roof glitter in the sun. The terrace and the temples looked much as they do now, except today the wooden structures are gone and only the stones remain.

Chou tells us that he saw the royal procession five or six times during his stay in Angkor. Although he was used to royal splendor in the Mongol court, he was still awed by the magnificent Khmer display. The king had been fitted out with iron armor and did not fear to show himself in public as Jayavarman VIII had. The procession was headed by a troop of horsemen riding small Mongolian ponies. They were followed by standard bearers holding aloft fluttering flags. Behind the flags came a band of flutes, conch horns, and drums.

Following the band were hundreds of girls from the 4,000 classical dancers the king kept in the palace. In addition to the abbreviated costumes depicted in the stone carvings of Angkor Wat and the Bayon, the girls wore garlands of flowers about their heads. Each carried a lighted candle even though the sun was shining.

Behind the dancing girls came serving women from the palace. They carried utensils, weapons, and ornaments that the king might require.

Chou tells us that the splendor increased as the parade moved along: "Following the women of the palace are men-at-arms bearing lances and shields for they are the soldiers of the palace guard.

"In their wake come horse chariots and royal carriages all of gold and pulled by bulls. Behind them are elephants on which ride the nobles and ministers of the government and princes of the realm. Each rides beneath a red parasol."

Next in line were the king's five wives. The principal wife— probably the one who betrayed her brother and stole the sacred sword to make her husband king—lived in the main palace in an apartment adjoining the king. She rode in a "tower" atop an elephant. The four lesser queens traveled in golden carts. We are told by Chou that they lived in individual palaces at north, south, east, and west corners of the city. All the queens were sheltered by golden umbrellas.

"The king himself comes last," Chou wrote, "standing on an elephant and holding in his hand the sacred sword. He is protected by horsemen and soldiers on elephants who crowd closely about him as the caravan proceeds through the city." For short trips between palaces and temples, the king was carried by palace girls in a golden planquin. But this stately procession accompanied him when he traveled any distance.

The sacred sword is the Prah Kahn which still remains today as the symbol of the realm. It is believed to be the "lightning of the god Indra" and no king can be coronated without it. At one time a Khmer king's ascent to the throne was delayed for several years because the Siamese had captured the sacred relic. To this day the sword is guarded by *baku* priests, and their care of it is unchanged from the days of Angkor. It is kept in the royal treasury except when removed for use by the king on special occasions. Legend claims that great calamity will befall the sons of Kambu if the blade is withdrawn from its golden scabbard without proper Sivaic rites. At periodic intervals it is removed and polished; it is the empire's soul and it must be kept perfect. A single speck of rust on it is a blot on the nation and every Khmer who ever lived.

Although he tried, Chou was not permitted to enter the palace itself. "I have been told," he wrote, "that the marvels of the inside are without number, but I have not seen them myself. The palace is well guarded and the sentries kept me out."

The inquisitive ambassador, however, did manage to enter the royal council chamber where Indravaraman gave his audiences. The council hall was in a special wooden building. As a building material, rock was reserved for the gods, and only temples were made of stone. Not even the king could live in a house of stone until after he was dead.

Chou tells us that the high tiled roof was supported from within by columns covered with burnished metal mirrors. For the audience the Chinese ambassador was seated on the floor with the Khmer and other state attendees. In front of them was a closed curtain. Offstage there was the sound of music from the drums and xylophones, which can still be heard today accompanying the traditional Khmer and Siamese dances.

At a signal blown from unseen conch horns, two scantily clad dancing girls ran out and raised the curtain to reveal the king. He posed in a gold-framed window with the Prah Kahn glittering in his hand. The audience put their hands together in a prayerful attitude of respect and bowed until their heads touched the floor. The mournful blasts of the conch horns continued for a short time. When they ceased, the audience sat up again.

The king sat upon a throne and motioned for the audience to begin. Petitioners usually spoke from their seats in the chamber, but if the petitioner was in special favor with the king he was permitted to approach the throne and sit on a lion's skin spread beside the king. Since lions are not native to Cambodia, presumably the skin was brought from abroad, and permission to sit upon it was considered a mark of great royal favor.

Some of the 4,000 dancing girls were also permitted to watch the royal audiences. Chou says they sat on a veranda raised above the hall and would peek around at the strange-looking Chinese visitors. He did not mind the impertinence, he says, for it also permitted him to look at them.

At the end of the audience, the two dancing girls returned to pull the curtain and the king was not seen again. According to Chou, Indravaraman held two such audiences daily to handle matters of state. Thus it appears that Indravarman was not merely a figurehead. He personally had the final word, not only on matters of state but also in the matter of justice. The king was the chief judge, and there was no appeal from his decisions. Apparently he even heard small disputes as well as more important matters.

According to Chou, at one time—probably when Buddhism was first introduced—the levying of fines was the only punishment. As the incidence of crime continued and even grew, however, the king resorted to flogging, a punishment everyone understood and feared. For the more serious crimes, the victim suffered loss of a member of his body. Thievery was punished by cutting off a finger, a hand, or even an arm. An habitual criminal was marked by the cutting off of all his toes; such a person was not permitted to enter the city gates, but was forced to live outside.

In criminal cases, judging was trial by ordeal. The suspect was forced to plunge his hand in burning oil; if he was not burned, he was declared innocent. In the old days the priests of Siva stuck their own hands in the oil before the victim. They were not burned, and this proved to the populace that the judging was fair. The trick was in knowing how. The priests often applied grease before plunging their hands into the oil. This grease prevented the oil from sticking to their hands and burning them.

In civil cases, testimony was heard, and the verdict favored the one who told the best story. When this was equal, the Khmers resorted to psychology. Across from the royal terraces are square towers known as the "Towers of the Rope Dancers." Most authorities deny that the towers could have been used by acrobats, as the name suggests. They say the towers are too high and widely spaced for that. Regardless of any other use the towers may have had, they served in the administration of justice. For when it was not possible to decide between two conflicting witnesses, both were taken and shut up in separate towers. Here, in the darkness, amid the effigies of the gods, they were left to commune with their consciences. Chou said the innocent suffered no ill effects, but that the guilty broke out in boils or fevers within five days. With what we know about psychosomatic disorders today—it is logical to suppose that such a system worked with more than a fair degree of accuracy.

One of the odder monuments mentioned by Chou is the Phimeanakas. It still stands today and reminds one of the temples of the Mayans of Central America. Chou had quite a story to tell about this monument. As previously noted, the land of the Khmers was created when the *naga* king drank the gulf water to provide land for his beloved daughter's kingdom when she married the mortal prince. A new legend takes up where the original one leaves off.

The snake princess was immortal. When her husband, Kambu, founder of Kambuja, died, she decided to remain with his people because of her undying love for him. She could not, of course, be subordinated to any other woman in the realm. Therefore, she insisted that each succeeding king marry her and that he visit her each night. If he missed a single night's visit, terrible things would happen to him and to the kingdom. By day she was a seven-headed cobra like her father, but at night she turned into the beautiful girl who charmed the first king of the Khmers.

Legends often reveal a factual beginning if one can go back far enough. It is possible that the legend Chou heard is not ancient at all, but an allegory. It could be the story of the usurper Indravarman and his queen, related in a legendary manner to keep the storyteller from being executed. If this is true, the legendary snake princess in this tale is really the queen who stole the sacred sword to help her husband steal the throne from her brother when her father died. In return for this treachery, she occupied a position unusual for a woman in an eastern country. Chou says that in the processions she rode an elephant that lifted her higher than anyone else, and, even more unusual, he says she sat beside the king at the royal audiences. There is no precedent for this in Angkorean history.

In general, women had a much freer existence in Cambodia than in China, Chou discovered. For example, they did most of the trading in the marketplaces. His account sounds like a modern travel writer's description of village markets today.

Business started early in the morning, when it was still cool, and ceased at noon. Every small merchant had her own place. Each morning she spread out her mat and put out her goods. A multitude of products were available—food, live animals, clothing, silverwork, rice wine, and rum made from sugar cane. No money was used, although money was known. Trade was by barter. Rice was a favorite medium of exchange, but the stall merchants would take in payment anything they thought they could trade.

Chou quickly found that these Cambodian women could match the traditional sharpness of the Chinese at trading. Sometimes they proved too sharp. "There have been also such as cheat the Chinese," he complained.

By this time Chinese were no novelty in Angkor Thom. Trading vessels and caravans made regular trips between the two countries. In the homes of upper class Cambodians, Chinese porcelain had taken the place of clay bowls, and low Chinese tables had come into fashion. Chinese beds were being introduced into wealthy homes, although the common people still slept on bamboo mats.

Many Chinese traders and coolies from trading vessels settled in Angkor. They told Chou it was because "rice is easy to get and so are wives, houses and a business to get on with." These newcomers soon found they were no match for the sharp-trading Cambodian women. All married as quickly as possible to get wives who could trade for them.

CHAPTER 7

****

THE FALL
OF ANGKOR

NOW, WITH THE hindsight of history, some modern historians say
that when Chou Ta-kuan visited Angkor Thom the great city was
already in a state of decline. But Chou's account does not indicate
this. According to it, Angkor was living on its past and present
glory, and its people were happy.

The carvings on the Bayon walls show that the people had plenty
to amuse themselves. One bas relief shows a cock fight. The owners
are on their knees holding their bristling birds; eager watchers
crowd about them. Two of them have their hands out, as if making
bets; one is smiling, the other is wearing a frown. Another carving
depicts what must have been a wild boar fight. Huge hogs are restrained by harnesses held by their trainers. Another relief shows

a clear rendition of a snake charmer bringing a cobra out of a pot.

Acrobatics must have been a very popular amusement, too, since acrobats appear often in the Bayon carvings. One carving shows a man on his knees, holding a child standing on one leg in each of his hands. Next to him another man lies on his back, spinning an ox wheel with his feet. Another seems to be balancing a pole on his head. Farther down the line two young contortionists are doing their act on top of a pole. Another relief shows a row of drums on the ground with a child or dwarf beating out a tune by dancing on their tops.

Hunting scenes were popular. Some reliefs show hunters stalking game with poisoned darts while others are armed with spears and bows. It seems that hunting was not always fun. In one relief an unfortunate man has just been cut in half by a crocodile.

Other scenes show open-air markets exactly like those Chou described. Farmers, cooks, and porters are represented in others. One stone scene shows men making brick; in another cutters are dressing rock to build another temple.

When Chou left Angkor the curtain of mystery slowly started to fall around the doomed city, and progress came to a halt. The practice of carving the king's accomplishments on stone was stopped. As a result there are no records of these declining years. If anything was written on material other than stone, it was destroyed by the jungle rot as was everything else in Angkor that was not made of stone. It is almost as if the Khmers were ashamed of their great nation's decay and wished to hide it from the world.

All we know of these declining years comes from fragments in the annals of Cambodia's neighbors, and these cannot always be trusted. By their very nature they are biased in favor of their own side. One thing is certain, however: they were years of almost constant warfare. We can obtain a good idea of the way the battles were fought from the pictures carved on the Bayon walls. The battle scenes are ferocious. Soldiers with round shields hurl them-

*A tree seed settles itself on top of a stone temple and sends its roots
down to the ground. That is how the jungle destroyed Angkor
Thom.*

selves at the enemy, while the cavalry fights from the backs of elephants. The king himself fights from a howdah on an elephant. The battle begins with a long-range attack by crossbows, then changes to hand-to-hand combat with javelin and sword. The elephants crash together like giant animated tanks.

Indravarman, whom Chou knew, reigned only another eleven years after Chou returned to the Mongol court. There is evidence that the king abdicated in 1308 for unknown reasons and was succeeded by a cousin, Indrajayavarman.

There has been an attempt to connect Indravarman with a curious Cambodian folk tale called "The King of the Sweet Cucumbers." It tells of a gardener who grew the best cucumbers in the world. The king thought them the most delicious food he had ever tasted and commanded the gardener to grow them exclusively for the royal table. He also gave the gardener a spear to use in protecting the garden. One night the king grew hungry and went to the cucumber field. The gardener, thinking him a thief, drove the spear into the intruder. The royal councillors pondered the slaying the next day and decided the king's death by his own spear was a sign from the gods. They married the gardener to the king's daughter and made him the new king.

This tale is supposed to be a veiled version of Indravarman's murder of Jayavarman's heir and his marriage to the old king's daughter. The story was believed to have so much truth in it that for a long time it was included in Cambodian school history books. There was also a street in Phnom Penh named, in reference to the tale, "The Street of the Sweet Cucumbers."

The empire was on the decline. However, so powerful a nation never dies overnight. The end comes slowly, and Angkor was another hundred years in dying.

During this declining century, the empire shrank gradually as, one by one, the conquered provinces regained their independence. Once free, they turned to attack their former Khmer masters. The most ferocious of these were the Thais (Siamese). After the Thais conquered the Mons following their migration from China, they were in turn conquered by the Khmers. Then, as Angkor weakened, the Thais grew stronger and their fights with the Cambodians more devastating. From 1350 on there was continual war between the two nations. It continued almost without interruption until the French established a protectorate over Cambodia in the nineteenth century.

While Cambodia was fighting the Thais on its northwestern border, the Laotians were building their nation from Cambodia's northern province. The Chams, driven out of their country by the Annamites, moved into Cambodia's Mekong delta area. Cambodia's enemies were squeezing in from every side.

Finally, in 1430 the Thais were strong enough to sweep through the Khmer outposts and put Angkor Thom under siege. The Khmer king died during the seven-month siege. As usual, there was a power struggle for the throne. Disgruntled members of the losing party turned traitors and opened the city gates to the invaders.

When the slaughter ceased, the Thais made Prince Intaburi, son of the Siamese king, the new ruler of the Khmers. It was only a short time before a Khmer assassin ended his reign.

The Cambodians massed to renew the battle. The Thais decided it was futile to try to hold the country. They retreated after sacking Angkor of every movable treasure they could strip from the city. The booty included the king's 4,000 dancing girls. Their exile to Siam ended classical dancing in Cambodia. Two hundred years later descendants of these girls would be brought back to revive the Khmer dances in the land of its birth.

When the Thais left, the Cambodians crowned Ponhea Yat as their new king. He apparently ruled in Angkor for only a year. Then he led the people on the sudden and inexplicable flight from the city. Angkor was completely deserted and left to the jungle. The accounts of its glory passed into legend.

Many reasons have been given for the Khmers' desertion of Angkor. But Miloslav Krasa, in *The Temples of Angkor,* is one of the few to give a totally honest answer: "Even today we cannot say with certainty what was the real cause of the desertion of Angkor. No preserved historical evidence says a word about it." Nobody knows. All explanations are only conjecture. Many theories that fit the facts have evolved over the years, but every one has flaws that fail to explain all the mystery.

One belief is that Angkor was abandoned because it was too exposed to future Thai attacks. It seems unlikely that this could be true. Angkor was well fortified. The Thais were never successful in storming the city's walls. The city fell to the Thais only because of traitors in the Angkorean ranks.

Also, there is the fact that the capital was moved to Oudong, which is 20 miles up-river from the present site of Phnom Penh. But if the fleeing Khmers were seeking a safe place to build their new capital, they picked a strange one. Twice—once with the Javanese and once with the Chams—the river afforded invaders a road into Cambodia.

It also does not seem reasonable to desert so great a city just because it had been sacked once. Jayavarman II came back to Yasodharapura after it had been totally destroyed by the Chams to rebuild it into Angkor.

And, even if Ponhea Yat did consider it necessary to move his capital for security reasons, was it necessary to turn Angkor Thom into a ghost city? The capital was not the only city in the Khmer realm. Although many people would be forced to follow the court, did all have to leave? Why didn't anyone, even a few people, remain in the capital? It was certainly not because they feared the Thais. There were numerous Khmer towns and villages between Angkor and the Thai border which were not deserted, as far as we know.

Another theory is that Angkor was destroyed by a revolt of its slaves. Novelist Peter Bourne based his plot for *When God Slept* on this theory. The trouble with this theory is that Angkorean building had ceased long before the city was abandoned. There were no hordes of construction slaves. Also Kambuja's poor military showing for the previous hundred years make it unlikely that they had large masses of slaves. Anyway, the sacking of Angkor by the Thais the previous year would have given slaves a chance to escape.

Still another reason given for the city's abandonment is the possibility that a great plague hit the city. This seems logical. The people would have viewed the deaths as a sign of divine disfavor. Then Angkor would have been abandoned in superstitious fear. The only thing wrong with this theory—possible though it may be—is that there is not one single bit of evidence to support it. It is pure speculation.

We are also told that the country's decline was possibly the result of the feverish building and the wars of Jayavarman VII. The great king left the country mighty, but physically exhausted. If so, the people must have been the most tired race in history, for while Jayavarman died in 1215, Angkor Thom was abandoned in 1432, making the time between the supposed exhaustion of the people and the fall 217 years, or longer than the history of the United States as a nation. One will be forgiven for thinking that no matter how tired Jayavarman left his people, they should have been able to replenish their energies in 217 years.

The most widely accepted theory today places the blame on religious influence. At different times, Sivaism, Vishnuism, and Buddhism, respectively, ruled as the national religion. The original Khmer Buddhism made a god of Buddha. Thus, the great Jayavarman VII was able to personify himself as the Buddha-raja —or Buddha king-god—in the multitude of faces he raised in the stones of the Bayon.

However, a hundred years later when Chou Ta-kuan visited Angkor he commented on the fact that there had been a definite shift from the Buddhism of Jayavarman's day to what has become known as the Little Vehicle of Buddhism, or Hinayana Buddhism.

Both religions drew their inspiration from Prince Siddartha of India who renounced the pleasures of his father's court to become a wandering monk. Through study and meditation he eventually became a Buddha, which means an Enlightened One. At this stage, he passed into Nirvana which, in Buddhism, meant that his soul has become one with the supreme spirit.

Hinayana Buddhism regards the Buddha as the ideal man, but still a man. It is an austere religion recognizing no gods and insisting that man's salvation can come only from himself. There is no priesthood, but rather a community of monks.

Many historians believe that the growth of this religion in Cambodia brought about a change of national character. Before, the king was the manifestation of the country's god—whether he happened to be Siva, Vishnu, or Buddha. Hinayana Buddhism recognizes no god. Therefore the people ceased to follow blindly a god-king who was just another man like themselves.

Louis Finot, the French archeologist, put it this way: "This religion was economical, its ministers pledged to poverty, contenting themselves with a straw roof and a bowl of rice. It was a moral religion whose principles assured peace of soul and social tranquility." Finot believed that the Khmer people, worn out by war and the expenditure of the nation's wealth on temples to false gods, were happy to embrace this new religion that took no interest in worldly things and faced trouble with resignation.

Georges Coedés, who was a long time with the museum in Phnom Penh, echoes this theory: "This Buddhism without deities, so different from the Buddhism of Jayavarman VII, could not but destroy the cult which forced the people to worship the king-god. Very probably this new faith played an important part in the rapid decline of the Khmer nation in the Fourteenth Century."

Although this theory may be valid, and Hinayana Buddhism did play a major part in the decline of the Khmers, it does not explain the abandonment of Angkor Thom itself.

The only logical assumption is that something so shocking happened in Angkor as to make both the Khmers and their enemies afraid to live in the city any longer. Whatever it was caused everyone to abandon one of the world's great cities.

What it was no one knows.

Neither is it known whether Angkor was abandoned in a day, a month, or within a year, Not a single documentary reference or even a legend has survived to describe the exodus. More than a million people left, and the jungle was permitted to take over. Vegetation springs up fast in the jungles. The city was quickly hidden while jungle rot attacked everything but the stone, which in turn was attacked by the fromager trees. Seeds blown by the wind or dropped by birds lodged in cracks atop the temples. Swiftly, snaking roots entwined to either knock the stones apart, as they did at the Bayon, or to completely imprison them, as in some cases in the temple called the Ta Prohn.

There is some evidence that Buddhist priests did from time to time live in Angkor Wat, the great temple outside Angkor Thom's city walls. However, even this was abandoned long before the coming of the first Europeans to the area. Angkor became a ghost city so completely screened by the jungle that one had to stumble upon it.

Although the Khmers never returned to Angkor Thom nor even built villages near it for over 400 years, the memory remained with them. Occasionally mention of the lost city would crop out in tales told to Europeans who refused to believe them until the sceptical Henri Mouhot astounded Europe with proof that there was indeed a lost city hidden in the Indochinese jungle.

CHAPTER 8

****

THE BITTER YEARS

IN THE YEARS following the abandonment of Angkor Thom, the Khmers were not the only nation facing extinction. The Chams were in even more trouble. In 1471 the Annamities stormed the Cham capital at Vijaya, and the desperate defenders begged the Khmers for help in fighting their common enemy.

Unfortunately, Cambodia was split between rival kings and also faced another war with the Thais. She could not help the Chams and Champa was unable to stop Annam alone. The Chams were reduced first to a vassal principality and then disappeared forever as a nation.

Although Champa was destroyed, the Chams themselves kept up enough revolts to keep Annam too busy to attack Kambuja for the next fifty years. With the Khmer flank thus protected, King

Ang Chan built up Cambodian strength. First in 1510, and again in 1524, he smashed Thai attacks. For a short time during his reign it appeared as though Cambodia was on the road back to glory. When Ang Chan died, he left the country in its best shape since the fall of Angkor more than a hundred years before.

Ang Chan's son Barom Racha was even more successful. In 1556 Siam suffered a disastrous invasion by Burma on her Western frontier. Racha took advantage of the Burmese coup and attacked Siam himself. He took 70,000 prisoners and regained all the provinces Cambodia had lost to Siam in the last 125 years.

When it began to appear that the Khmers were on the road to regaining their former glory, Racha died. He was the last strong king. At his death, disunity once more split the country, giving Siam an opportunity to retake two of the lost provinces.

In 1580 Chey Chetta I was crowned king of Cambodia, despite the objections of a powerful minority. Beset as he was by enemies from within and without, the king was taken in by Diego Bellosa of Portugal, a European adventurer. In view of Bellosa's later actions, it is possible that he told the king that he was related to the Spanish viceroy of the Philippine Islands and could get military aid to help Chey Chetta.

In a short time Bellosa became the king's favorite and the husband of a royal princess. He began to dream of becoming prime minister and later—through his royal wife—perhaps even king. Unfortunately, his steady progress toward this goal was interrupted by another Siamese invasion, in 1583. A year later the Cambodian capital fell and the king and his two sons fled into what is now Laos.

Bellosa escaped to Manila where he tried to get the Spanish viceroy to send soldiers to Cambodia. He had a good argument, but it would have infuriated his royal Cambodian friend. Bellosa pointed out how easy it would be for trained Spanish troops to drive out the "barbarians" and take possession of Cambodia for the King of Spain. Then he, Bellosa, would be delighted to serve as viceroy.

The Spanish refused to act. The Malays in the southern Philippines were in revolt and the viceroy had no troops to spare. The disappointed adventurer went back to Cambodia, not knowing that his royal protector was in exile and that a new man, King Ream, sat on the Khmer throne. Bellosa was thrown into prison, but his "audacious lies," as one Cambodian historian put it, soon had him out again. He convinced King Ream that the Spanish were getting ready to intervene in the war on the Siamese side.

Alarmed, the king was persuaded to appoint Bellosa as his envoy to Manila to persuade the Spanish to remain neutral. This time Bellosa found a new viceroy, Luis Perez de la Marinas, who also refused help. Then Bellosa enlisted the aid of an order of Dominican monks by convincing them that they could convert the Khmer king to Christianity. The monks put so much pressure on de la Marinas that he gave Bellosa three manned ships. The story does not tell the size of the ships, but they must have been small for Bellosa had only thirty-eight men under his command when he sailed back to Cambodia.

The vessels ran into a storm and one was separated from the others. Bellosa went on up the Mekong without it. As a ruse to avoid suspicion until he could spring a surprise attack, he claimed to be heading a trading party. This claim turned out to be worse than a frank declaration of war. The Chinese colony, which had been in Cambodia since the days of Chou Ta-kuan, was the dominant force in the country's business. Fearing that the Spanish had come to break their trade monopoly, the Chinese started a riot. When they swept down to the dock to burn Bellosa's ships, he slaughtered 300 of them with his cannon. Bellosa then tried to see the king, but the palace was barred to him. His presents, including the first donkey ever seen in Cambodia, were refused. The angry adventurer set fire to the palace and started a battle in which the king was killed. Bellosa was unable to maintain his position with his small force, and when the missing ship turned up suddenly, he was glad to flee on it.

The ship headed back to Manila, but Bellosa did not return

with it. He still dreamed of turning Cambodia into a private kingdom for himself. He had the ship's captain drop him and a companion, Blas Ruiz, along the Annam coast. The two adventurers then made a heroic march over the mountains into Laos in search of the exiled former king, Chey Chetta, who had first befriended Bellosa. They found that he had died. Undaunted, Bellosa took Chey Chetta's surviving son, Ponhea Yat, and by treachery, guile, and gall restored him to the Khmer throne.

The grateful king rewarded Bellosa and Ruiz by making them governors of two provinces. Unfortunately for the ambitious Europeans, the provinces had a large number of Chams in their populations who had immigrated to Cambodia after Annam destroyed Champa. The Chams were extremely devout Moslems and violently hated Christianity, and the news that their governors were Catholics threw the Chams into an uproar. The trouble grew worse with a rumor that the governors intended to force the Chams to turn Christian. An immediate revolt broke out. Bellosa and Ruiz were unable to put it down and the king either could not or would not help them.

Bellosa again fled to Manila and returned with six ships manned by dock scum he recruited by describing the gold to be found in Cambodia. The ships sailed up the Mekong where they were attacked by a combined force of Chams, Malays, and Chinese. Bellosa, Ruiz, and all their forces were slaughtered. The year was 1599.

As the years went by, the Khmer nation was the continual prey of Siam and Annam. The struggle of these two nations to annex Cambodia continued through the first thirty years of the nineteenth century. In 1833 the Annamites were finally strong enough to drive out the Siamese and put their puppet King Ang Chan on the Khmer throne. An army of occupation was left in Cambodia to keep out the Thais and to insure the puppet's loyalty to Annam. Ang Chan died the following year and was succeeded by his daughter. However, she was a queen in name only, and the occupation general added her to his harem and set about annexing Cambodia to Annam.

This was one of the darkest hours in Khmer history. The Khmers' last hope of remaining a nation lay with Ang Chan's two brothers, Ang Em and Ang Duong. The brothers tried to rally the Khmers, but could not get sufficient support. They tried to fight anyway, but their small army was quickly smashed. Ang Em was captured by the Annamites and Ang Duong fled to Siam.

In this moment of supreme crisis, help came from the least expected source, the Buddhist *bonze,* as the monks were called. Historians have often blamed Hinayana Buddhism, with its doctrine of resignation, as the chief reason for the Khmer decline. However, the actions of the monks in this crisis showed that the *bonze* were capable of decisive action when their religion was threatened. The Annamites had no use for the Hinayana sect. The monks expected the Annamites to try to destroy their faith if Cambodia was absorbed into Annam.

This certainty—and probably a stirring of dormant pride in their race—caused the monks to organize a revolt. They went everywhere, trudging down jungle paths and up mountain trails, preaching that the invaders were set upon destroying both the sons of Kambu and their gods. In the jungle villages, rice farmers, hunters, and fishermen who had paid scant attention to intrigue and war now started to rally behind the militant monks.

Small guerrilla bands were formed throughout Cambodia. Comprised of villagers, each was independent with no central leader. They fell upon the Annamites whenever they could, then they hid their weapons and went back to their rice paddies until another opportunity arose.

The Annamites fought back, but were at a disadvantage. There was no regular army for them to fight. While this harassment was continuing, Cambodian royalists sent a petition to Siam asking King Rama III to intervene. The Siamese were happy to comply. They drove out the Annamites and put Prince Ang Doung on the

Khmer throne. The coronation, in 1847, was held in Bangkok, Siam, as a reminder to the new Khmer king he owed his throne and allegiance to Siam. And during the first part of his reign Ang Doung had to ask Thai permission for every act. The Khmers had only substituted one foreign master for another.

By the middle of the nineteenth century, European countries were building colonial empires in Asia. Russia and England were trying to dismember China. The Dutch were enlarging their holdings in Indonesia. England was grabbing Singapore and India. France, not to be outdone, was building a colonial empire in Southeast Asia.

Soon Siam (later Thailand) was the only really independent country left. King Mongkut (of *Anna and the King of Siam* fame) shrewdly kept Siam independent by pitting the greed of England and France against each other. France, in the meantime, sent missionaries into Annam and then used their persecution as an excuse for sending in troops. By 1859 France was in complete control of the Annamite country which now comprises South Vietnam. It was land that Annam had previously taken from the Chams.

In the meantime, King Ang Doung of Cambodia sent a letter to Napoleon III of France asking for protection from Siam. He did this in the hope that it would involve France, Siam, and England in a three-way struggle that would permit Cambodia to escape from its Siamese overlordship. King Mongkut, learning of the letter, threatened to send an occupation army to Oudong, the Cambodian capital, and Ang Doung hastily withdrew his petition to Napoleon III.

Later, when England and France were almost at war over their individual ambitions in Asia, Ang Doung once more tried to move into the French orbit. Before anything could come of this new attempt to break away from Siamese control, Ang Doung died. He was succeeded by his son Norodom who was ousted by a revolution.

Norodom fled to Siam where he complained to Mongkut that the revolt was French inspired. Mongkut sent a Siamese army that put down the revolt. Norodom was crowned King of the Khmers in 1862. Because he owed his throne to the Siamese, he dropped his father's advances to the French.

In the meantime, France had been steadily gobbling up Annam. French missionaries and explorers were busy roaming through the jungles of Cambodia, Laos, and Tonkin in preparation for further colonial expansion.

A priest was the first to find Angkor, but his report was regarded as an exaggeration. Then, when Henri Mouhot's excitedly written scientific report reached Europe, French interest in Cambodia increased. An elaborate expedition headed at first by Naval Commander Doudart de Lagree and then by Lieutenant Francis Granier was sent into Cambodia and Laos, penetrating as far north as the Chinese border. The engravings made by the expedition's artist, Louis de la Porte, created a sensation. After this it was but a matter of time before the French would move into Cambodia.

After the final conquest of Annam, France made elaborate plans for a completely new nation which it would call French Indochina. The delta area Annam had seized from Cambodia became Cochin-China. Laos, Tonkin, and Annam (Vietnam) all became part of the new colonial empire. The next step was to bring Cambodia into French Indochina.

To this end Doudart de Lagree came from French headquarters in Saigon to visit King Norodom at Oudong in 1863. He reminded the king that the late King Ang Doung had sought French protection. In addition, he claimed that since Cambodia had been conquered by Annam, it now rightly belonged to France anyway.

"However, France has no intention of asserting its rightful claim," de Lagree assured the alarmed king. "We wish only to be of service to Your Majesty in preventing Siam from absorbing Cambodia. In accordance with the wishes of his late majesty, King Ang Doung, we will establish a protectorate over Cambodia. We will not interfere in your country's internal affairs. We will only assure protection from foreign aggression."

This move infuriated Siam, which was exercising an overlordship over Cambodia, issuing orders to King Norodom. The Siamese king appealed to Sir John Bowring, the British diplomat, who was then in Siam trying to arrange a trade treaty. As a result, there was grave danger of a war between France and England over France's attempt to annex Cambodia.

To forestall trouble, de Lagree went to Bangkok for a conference with Bowring. The two reached an agreement permitting France to establish a protectorate over Cambodia. There were three conditions: France would guarantee Siam's independence; Siam could keep the three Cambodian provinces, including Angkor, which she occupied; and Cambodia would remain a separate country and not be absorbed into the Indochina state France was forming with Laos, Annam, and Tonkin.

Norodom was bitter. He felt he had only exchanged Siamese masters for French ones, and time proved him right. In 1888, France forced a new treaty on Cambodia which reduced Norodom to a figurehead. French officials were placed in charge of all government posts above village headman. Frenchmen controlled the army and police. French judges had to be members of all courts and no Frenchman could be tried in a Khmer court.

In 1907, when all danger of England supporting the Thais was past, France forced Siam to cede the Cambodian provinces she had taken earlier, including the ruins of Angkor Thom. Immediately scientists from the French School of the Far East took over the lost city. After the jungle was cleared away, they began a painstaking restoration of the temples.

During their overlordship of Cambodia, the French built roads, public buildings, and hospitals, but deliberately neglected development of schools. They knew from experience that educating natives only prepared future revolutionists. As a result, young Cambodians, except for a few of the royal family, received no schooling beyond the elementary studies in village pagodas.

King Norodom lived out his reign as an unhappy prisoner of the French. There was one attempt to overthrow French rule, but it was quickly suppressed. When Norodom died his son was expected to succeed him, but the French intervened. The king's brother Prince Sisowath, who had helped the French during the abortive revolution, was given the throne as his reward.

Sisowath, now king, did exactly as he was told throughout his own reign, and caused his French "protectors" no trouble. When he died in 1927, supporters of the Norodom family expected the crown to be returned to them, as members in the direct line of succession. But they were disappointed. The French still did not trust the Norodom family and forced the royal council to crown Sisowath's son, Monivang.

This further widened the breach between the Norodom and Sisowath branches of the royal family. Many thought it would lead to open war, as had happened often in Cambodia's past, but the expected revolution did not come. Neither side could muster sufficient strength to bring about a civil war. The French settled back, pleased. The important thing was to have a king they could control, and they believed Monivang was he.

As it happened, he was not.

CHAPTER 9

****

SIHANOUK

THE FRENCH HAD always gone out of their way to foster respect for the king. Despite the inroads of the Hinayana religion, which denied the king's divine origin, awe of the monarch had never been completely effaced. This was to France's advantage: since the king was under its control, the people were less likely to revolt.

The French insisted that the king live and look like a Khmer monarch, even though they did not permit him to act like one. In 1915 they built a sumptuous royal palace designed in the Khmer architectural style. He was permitted to have fifty wives and two hundred dancing girls. His court in the capital of Phnom Penh glittered with barbaric splendor.

In exchange for worldly pleasures, the king was expected to

keep the country quiet under French rule. He could make no move without French approval. For twelve years Monivang was forced to play his puppet role. Then the outbreak of World War II changed the situation in Southeast Asia. In 1940, France fell to the German army and immediately trouble developed between French Indochina and Siam, with the Siamese supported by the Japanese.

Admiral Henri Decoux, the French governor of Indochina, suggested to Monivang that he raise a Khmer army to help protect his country. The king smiled. "But my people do not know how to fight," he said. "All they know how to do is sing and make love!"

The infuriated admiral could do nothing. A native uprising would be disasterous for the French. There were only a small number of French troops left—many had been taken home to fight against Germany. Now the German-dominated Vichy government ruling France could not possibly send help if trouble developed. The French knew that Japan was only waiting for an excuse to move in and take all of France's possessions in the Far East. Monivang's reluctance to cooperate made the French officials fear that the king would start trouble to give the Japanese this excuse. Therefore, there was genuine relief in official circles when Monivang died on April 22, 1941.

Admiral Decoux, determined to maintain order in the face of rising trouble, refused to accept Monivang's son, Monireth, as king. Secret reports showed that the prince was even more independence minded than his 65-year-old father had been.

It was not difficult to stop Monireth from succeeding. In Cambodia the throne has never been hereditary. The oldest son did not automatically become king, as in European monarchies. Under Cambodian law and custom, a council of royal princes meet upon the death of the old king and elect the new one. The only requirement in modern times is that the candidate be of the direct blood line of King Ang Doung. Twice before the French had interceded to force the council to elect a king agreeable to the colonial government, and Decoux was determined to do it again. "The council will elect whomever I choose," he said positively.

The question was, who? All possible candidates were investigated. A detailed report was made of each man's actions, beliefs, associations, and history, and the dossier of each was carefully evaluated. One by one each candidate was eliminated. Finally, only one file remained, that of Prince Norodom Sihanouk.

The prince was a teen-ager, then attending a French academy in Saigon. Of all the candidates, he seemed the least likely to be king. According to all reports, he had never shown any interest in politics. He was interested in music. His instrument was the saxophone, which he played well, and he had a special fondness for American jazz and even composed some fair music himself. He was also interested in horses, especially jumpers. And he was said to have quite an eye for girls. His personality was amiable and he got along well with people.

"Excellent!" the admiral said as he laid down the file. "This young man has all the qualifications for a king—Cambodian style. Inform the Council that they *will* elect him."

No one was more surprised than Prince Norodom Sihanouk when he was recalled from Saigon and informed that he was the new king of the Khmers. In a few short years the French would be even more surprised. Such a man would find ways to amuse himself while French officials ran the country. They sought a weak king with playboy interests and got instead the greatest man of his race since the days of Jayavarman VII.

In the mountain, they felt that it was necessary to explain why the dead king's son had been passed over. In an official statement, Admiral Decoux reviewed the royal succession since King Ang Doung, which showed that there were two branches of the royal family, the Norodom branch founded by Ang Doung's oldest son and the Sisowath branch founded by the king's second son.

Norodom succeeded his father, but when he died in 1904 the council passed over his son and elected Prince Sisowath, the dead king's brother. The official explanation omitted the fact that this was done under French pressure.

Sisowath in turn was succeeded by his son Monivang, again passing up the Norodom branch which considered itself in the direct line of succession. At this point, Admiral Decoux noted that the election of King Sisowath following Norodom's death in 1904 started a quarrel between the two branches of the family that had continued to the present day.

"Now," the admiral said, "with the death of King Monivang, the council was most anxious to end the rivalry. For this reason it decided to elect someone who could end the rivalry. The perfect person has been found in Prince Norodom Sihanouk who was then attending school in Saigon. He is the great-great grandson of King Ang Doung and the great-grandson of King Norodom through his father. Through his mother, who is a Sisowath, he is also the great-grandson of King Sisowath. Thus in him the two rival lines of claimants to the throne are united."

For the first four years of his reign Sihanouk could do little more than be the sort of king the French expected. As World War II progressed, Japan occupied Thailand and British Malaya. She did not attack the French in Cambodia because Japan and Germany were allies and Germany controlled France through the puppet Vichy government. This changed suddenly when American and British forces invaded France on D-Day in 1944. France was quickly liberated and the pro-German Vichy government replaced with a Free French cabinet.

Japan, suspecting that Germany now would lose the war, moved swiftly to consolidate her position in Southeast Asia. On March 5, 1945, Japan struck swiftly at all French positions in Indochina. The entire French colonial staffs were removed. Laos, Vietnam and Cambodia were invited by Japan to declare their independence from France, which King Sihanouk did on March 12, 1945. The Japanese occupation force then brought Son Ngoc Thanh, a Cambodian rebel exiled earlier by the French, back from Japan. Thanh had been fighting for Cambodian independence since 1936 and was tremendously popular. Following Japanese suggestions, Sihanouk appointed Son Ngoc Thanh prime minister.

Although they were conquerors, the Japanese were careful not to offend the Cambodians. They asserted the fiction that they came as liberators, interested only in aiding all Asians to throw off the colonial yoke of their European masters. They spoke glowingly of the important place Cambodia would have in the Asian co-prosperity sphere which Japan would organize.

Such a fiction was necessary because Japan could not afford the troops necessary to put down any native rebellions in Indochina. American forces were moving closer to Japan. United States planes were pounding Tokyo with fire-bomb raids, and the country expected its home islands to be invaded by General Douglas MacArthur.

In August, 1945, all Japanese plans for Indochina ended with the dropping of the atom bombs on Hiroshima and Nagasaki. Japan surrendered. Twenty days later French paratroopers were back in Saigon. The following month they took control of Phnom Penh and arrested Son Ngoc Thanh for collaborating with the Japanese.

King Sihanouk was not accused because the French needed his royal prestige to avoid trouble in Cambodia. Although the Laotians and Vietnamese were threatening to revolt, Sihanouk was expected to be docile, as he was before the war.

Immediately after the arrest and deportation of Son Ngoc Thanh, Admiral Thierry d 'Argentieu, the French High Commissioner in Indochina, brought a carefully prepared proclamation for Sihanouk to sign. It denounced Son Ngoc Thanh as a traitor and proclaimed Cambodia's loyalty to France.

Apparently the king signed willingly. He and Thanh had not agreed on the future course for the Khmer fight for independence. Thanh was a born rebel, dedicated to fighting for his ideals. Sihanouk clearly saw that Cambodia could never win a fighting war with the French. The guerrilla warfare advocated by Son Ngoc Thanh would drag on for years, killing thousands without accomplishing anything except added misery for the people. Sihanouk wanted to achieve independence through bloodless negotiation. More important in the king's view, Thanh was suspected of working secretly with Communist forces. Sihanouk had no intention of exchanging one dictator for another.

There were many who did not agree with the king. Several thousand followers of Son Ngoc Thanh fled to the jungles to form the Khmer Issaraks—the Free Cambodians—and make war on the French.

For his part in signing the proclamation, the Japanese returned to Sihanouk the provinces they had given to Thailand. He also got the *modus vivendi*—a temporary arrangement pending settlement of a dispute—signed on January 7, 1946. This document of rights was intended as a token gesture to still Cambodian unrest. In effect, it gave Cambodia greater control of the internal functions of the country. However, native courts still could not try foreigners, and the French continued to control the army, foreign affairs, finance, and commerce.

The following year Sihanouk abolished the absolute monarchy and gave the country its first constitution. Provision was made for free elections, political parties, a national assembly, and revised courts.

This move toward demoracy did not, of course, interfere with the king's traditional authority. An official document distributed in English by the Cambodian government made this clear:

> The king is the supreme Head of the State and His person is sacred and inviolable. All powers emanate from Him, but are practiced in His name by the organisms prescribed by the Constitution.
>
> He summons the National Assembly and can dissolve it . . . chooses the President of the Council of Ministers and appoints him as well as the Ministers proposed by this president. He names the magistrates on proposal of the superior Council of Magistracy and has the right of pardoning and commutation of sentence.
>
> Lastly, He is the supreme Head of the Armed Forces of the Kingdom and He signs and ratifies the Treaties according to the vote of the National Assembly.

In summary, the ministers would govern the country, but the king would choose the ministers and approve or veto their actions.

Continued dissatisfaction and the beginning of the war against the French in Vietnam by the Viet Minh brought further concessions to the Cambodians. A treaty was signed in November, 1949, that permitted the Khmer king to negotiate his own foreign relations. Both the French and Sihanouk hailed this action as the beginning of true independence, although the government was still dominated by the French and the French army still controlled the country.

There was widespread opposition to the treaty in Cambodia. The Khmer Democrats, which had grown to be the largest political party in Cambodia, sided with Son Ngoc Thanh. They denounced the king's program of gradually achieving independence through negotiations. Their members in the Assembly refused to ratify the treaty, and their denunciations of Sihanouk increased when the French suffered new reverses in the Vietnam fighting.

Sihanouk met the opposition by dissolving the Assembly. He then attempted to put the treaty into force by proclamation. The French were worried by the unrest in Cambodia and began to wonder if the treaty gave too many concessions. It now appeared to them that Sihanouk could not control the opposition. They therefore tried to change some of the provisions to give France greater control of internal affairs, which infuriated those opposing the king.

At the same time, the Communist-led Viet Minh made several attacks from North Vietnam into Cambodia. Angry denunciations from Hanoi accused Sihanouk of betraying his country to the French. Conditions worsened, but France continued to support the king. The ministers, dissatisfied as they were with Sihanuok, knew that only the monarchy could prevent a revolution in Cambodia.

In an attempt to restore unity, Sihanouk called new elections. The dissident Democrats won a resounding victory. They immediately demanded that Sihanouk petition the French to permit Son Ngock Thanh's return from exile. Faced with continued defeats in Vietnam, the French High Commissioner reluctantly agreed. Thanh's return from exile provoked the largest public demonstration in Cambodian history. Newsmen estimated that 100,000 people lined the streets of Phnom Penh to welcome the exile home.

Thanh quickly showed that his years of exile had not changed him. He was for complete independence and ready to fight for it. The alarmed French realized they made a mistake in permitting him to return, and orders were issued for his arrest. Unable to escape by plane, Thanh fled into the jungles where he joined forces again with the Khmer Issaraks.

He immediately issued a denunciation of Sihanouk, calling him a French puppet. Bitterly, he reminded the people that King Sihanouk had done nothing at the end of the war when France gave Cochin-China, the rich Mekong delta that had formerly been Khmer territory, to Vietnam. Still worse for Sihanouk, Thanh organized a Committee for National Liberation, which immediately announced that it would make Cambodia a republic.

Although he was attacked from all sides, the king was hurt most by the best thing he had done for his country, providing better schools. Students, with their increasing understanding of international affairs, opposed the king and supported Son Ngoc Thanh and the Democrats. The educated Buddhist monks—supposedly completely divorced from politics—also sided with the Democrats. The Issaraks were growing stronger and Communist influences were gaining strength in the country. At this time more than three-fifths of the country was controlled by anti-royal forces.

Fighting desperately both for his throne and his country, the king lashed out against those who would force him into a war with the French. "They would have me open the door to the Viet Minh [Vietnamese Communists] so that in the name of freedom they can massacre the little people, burn our bridges, our homes, our temples, our schools, our cities!" Sihanouk cried in a bitter speech denouncing the revolutionists. "Is this patriotic? Is it an acceptable solution for a king worthy of the name?"

Answering the students, and their support of Son Ngoc Thanh, he said: "I say that the so-called Khmer heroes have never done anything constructive. They have only brought disorder, disunity and ruin to our country!"

That was in June, 1952. The French were greatly pleased. King Norodom Sihanouk was behaving just as they wanted a Cambodian king to behave.

However, their pleasure with the young king was to be of short duration. Within a few months the French colonials would be denouncing him, and angry newspapers in Paris would be calling him "the mad king of Cambodia."

CHAPTER 10

****

THE
UNCROWNED
KING

IN AN ATTEMPT to soften the rising unrest in his country, the king immediately wrote a message promising to achieve independence peacefully within three years.

His negotiations with local French officials were fruitless. In February of the next year he went to France to present his problems directly to Vincent Auriol, president of the French Republic. Auriol found excuses not to see him. Sihanouk wrote a long letter setting forth his position. It was ignored. Angry and bitter, the king wrote again. He bluntly referred to the worsening situation in Cambodia and to the "grave consequences" that were sure to follow.

This jarred the French who were already bogged down in a

losing war with the Vietnamese. They could not afford another in Cambodia. Auriol agreed to see Sihanouk. The French president listened carefully, but did not commit himself.

A short time later Sihanouk presented the government with a carefully drawn plan for his country's independence. Again he referred to threats of armed revolution if his plan was not accepted.

The French government was fast losing patience. One clique in the Associated States department, which is responsible for France's overseas possessions, argued that Sihanouk could not afford a fight. His country was already split between his supporters and those of Son Ngoc Thanh. A fight would permit his enemies to oust him and bring about the republic Thanh had promised. "He won't dare let a revolution happen," French officials argued. "It would cost his crown." Accepting this view, Auriol refused to negotiate further. Sihanouk was in a difficult position. He had promised to bring about independence by negotiation within three years. Although he still had two years left in which to make good his promise, there was now little hope that he would ever get anywhere in talks with French officials.

Still, Sihanouk refused to go along with those who called for armed rebellion. He wanted no part of guerrilla war. Vietnam was a perfect example of what he wanted to avoid. Unable to make any headway in France, he decided to try to stimulate world sympathy for Cambodia. He hoped that this would bring pressure on the French government to change its policy toward Cambodia. He began secretly to make plans to go to Canada. Jean Letourneau, Minister for the Associated States, heard of it and immediately called the king's uncle, Prince Monireth, for a sharp, three-hour interview.

Monireth was the late King Monivang's son and the one expected to succeed his father before the French forced the Council to choose Sihanouk. Letourneau tried to find out from Monireth what Sihanouk planned to do in Canada. The prince replied blandly that he did not know. Letourneau flew into a rage and bitterly accused the king of deliberately causing trouble, adding,

"His people obey him implicitly. It is up to him to control them!"

Monireth had no cause to love the French. He listened and smiled and said he was only the king's loyal subject, not his confidant. He had no idea what his majesty was going to do.

"Then I suggest you warn him to be careful," the French minister said. "His crown may be at stake!"

Sihanouk went to Canada and then to the United States. He talked for an hour with John Foster Dulles, the American Secretary of State. Dulles said the United States, which had fought a revolution for its own freedom, naturally supported freedom for other colonial countries. However, he doubted whether a totally free Cambodia would be strong enough to resist Communist aggression. "You need the French army to protect you," Dulles insisted.

Angered at the American Secretary of State, Sihanouk went to New York where he gave a long interview to the New York *Times.* In it he set forth all his arguments for independence and his indictment of the French administration in Indochina. The king's argument in the *Times,* an international newspaper read widely by diplomats, aroused considerable discussion and resulted in the agreement of Paris to reopen talks about Cambodian independence. The French, however, merely wanted to get negotiations under way. They had little intention of the negotiations developing into anything. Their proposals, released on May 9, 1953, were angrily rejected by Sihanouk.

In Phnom Penh in June, the bitter king released a royal declaration setting forth his grievances against France. France claimed that Cambodia, through the former French concessions was independent in everything except defense and that the French army was essential to its protection.

Sihanouk charged in return that Cambodia had no control over the army, judicial system, or police. In addition, the country's economic and monetary policy was also French controlled. This situation, he exclaimed, constituted a stranglehold upon his nation.

Countering French charges and United States fears that communism would take over if the French army pulled out, Sihanouk made another proposal. He asked for French guarantees that the Associated States—Laos, Vietnam and Cambodia—would be given full independence when the war in Vietnam ended. The French refused to answer the proposal.

For the next several days the king remained locked in his palace while he agonized over what to do. One thing was certain: he had to achieve independence or face the loss of his crown. He had made a definite promise to achieve independence by peaceful means within three years. If he failed to make good, the followers of Son Ngoc Thanh would surely rise up in revolt, the French would attempt to put it down, then the country would be split between the royalists, the revolutionists, and the French, all fighting each other in a three-way struggle that would destroy Cambodia.

Suddenly deciding on a course of action, Sihanouk abruptly announced his self-exile from his country. He went to Thailand, and the French press expressed pleasure that France was rid of the "mad king of Cambodia" who had been causing so much trouble. It quickly became apparent that Sihanouk's actions had been carefully thought out. As soon as he left, Cambodians began forming guerrilla bands. The king had been the only influence that restrained open warfare. With his restraining influence gone, an explosion was inevitable. A report was sent back to Paris by an alarmed colonial government that 400,000 Khmers had taken up arms.

In Thailand, Sihanouk was greeted by the figurehead king. The dictator, Marshal Pibul Songgram, however, refused to see him. Thailand had enough trouble without adding to them by harboring the controversial self-exiled king of Cambodia. Angered at the rejection, and realizing he could accomplish nothing in Thailand, Sihanouk returned to Cambodia. He still shunned the capital and stayed in a small cottage near Angkor Thom.

Throughout the nation, angry Khmers rallied to the support of their king. Now France was caught in a difficult position. The war against the Communist-led Viet Minh in North Vietnam was getting worse. France was close to defeat. She could not risk fighting another war in Cambodia. Reluctantly, the government of Joseph Daniels announced that France was prepared to give independence to all the Associated States of Indochina.

The accord was signed in Paris early in 1954. A short time later, on May 6, the French suffered a decisive defeat at Dien Bien Phu and lost North Vietnam to Ho Chi Minh's Communists. This resulted in a North Vietnam and a South Vietnam, which in turn led to the civil war between the two sectors which involved the United States.

After the accord was signed, many of the revolutionary Khmer Issaraks laid down their arms. The true nature of those who did not quickly became apparent; they were completely Communist dominated and helped a Viet Minh force when it invaded Cambodia from Laos. There were immediate outcries in France and the United States that this was what they expected. Sihanouk's mad drive for independence had caused him to lose everything in the Communist trap.

The king moved swiftly, before anyone could suggest foreign intervention. As the head of the armed forces, he personally took the field to fight as commander of his army. The Khmers would not fight their king and they deserted the rebel groups to join his forces. The Viet Minh withdrew.

With his international problems temporarily solved, the king began to face equally difficult internal problems. Earlier, with French approval, he gave the country a constitution and an elected assembly.

Unfortunately, probably because of the earlier French refusal to provide proper training for young people during the protectorate, the country was not ready for a democratic type of government. Twice the king had been forced to dissolve the assembly when the members spent more time fighting him and each other than in trying to solve the country's troubles.

After dissolving the Assembly in January, 1953, he ruled as an absolute monarch until after independence was assured. After the

French left, the situation did not improve. Sihanouk was pledged by the Geneva Conference of 1954 to hold general elections. It seemed certain that the dissident Democrats who had caused so much trouble in the previous assemblies would again come out ahead.

Sihanouk postponed the elections and advanced a plan to revise the government. As announced in February, 1955, it would abolish political parties. This, the king believed, would eliminate the internal struggle between political groups who thought only of party welfare. He proposed to appoint the cabinet himself. He insisted that the government would be a democracy since the assembly would be elected by the people. However, the Assembly would not have the power to overthrow the ministers appointed by the king. These and other restrictions on who could hold office caused an uproar among the politicians. For two weeks the battle raged. Then on March 2, 1955, in a radio broadcast, Sihanouk suddenly announced his abdication.

Sihanouk's enemies were no less stunned than his supporters. It was suggested that it might be a hollow threat, but the king's action was final. He nominated, and the Royal Council approved, the coronation of his father, Prince Suramarit, and his mother, Princess Kossamak, as king and queen of the Khmers.

In his abdication speech, Sihanouk said that he had tried to give the people a reform government, but was opposed by dishonest officials, politicians, and wealthy persons.

"I want to work at removing injustices, corruption and exploitation," he said. "It is my belief that such a task cannot be properly fulfilled by a reigning monarch.

"As a king it was difficult for me to keep informed. I could see only the flowers and hear the lies. The true face of the people was hidden from me."

His concluding statement in his public broadcast left no doubt about his future: "If I have abdicated, it is not to abandon my people but to save them from the democracy that is pressing them and to bring about the reforms which I have worked for."

In a later speech and in private conversations, Prince Sihanouk gave more detailed reasons. One was that a king's time was taken up with so many formal affairs that he had no time to work. Another reason was his belief that the king should be above partisan politics, but in an elected type of government it was impossible for the head of state not to align himself with one party or the other.

Immediately after abdication, he formed the *Sangkum Restr Niyum*—the People's Socialist Party. Then his father, the new King Suramarit, called for a general election in September, 1955. Sihanouk hit the campaign trail with all the enthusiasm of a professional politician. He carried his fight to the smallest villages, seeking votes and asking people to "look at the record" of what he had done. He accused the Democrats of aligning themselves with the Communists and promised to drive out the self-seekers and make the "little man" important.

The effect of the ex-king energetically campaigning at the grass roots was bewildering to his former subjects. To them he was still king. They had not understood his abdication speech.

"What is this voting?" an old villager asked.

"The Prince needs your help," he was told. "If you are for him, drop a white ball in the jar."

"But he is the *king*," the old man replied, bewildered. "The king does not have to *ask* my help. All he has to do is *tell* me."

An example of how the jungle people still associate the king with the king-god of Angkorean time was related by Malcolm MacDonald, the British diplomat. MacDonald told how on a trip up-country with Sihanouk when the prince held an audience one old farmer complained that his planting was being delayed by rain and asked if it could please be stopped.

Sihanouk explained patiently that he had no power over the rain. The old man looked at him disbelievingly. "But you are the *king!*" he said.

The election was a clean sweep for Sihanouk and his new party. The opposition Democrats claimed that they were harassed during the elections and that their public meetings were broken up by the Prince's followers. The International Control Commission, set up to supervise the elections under the Geneva Agreement which ratified Cambodia's independence, investigated the Democrats' charges and ruled that the elections had been free and honest. Sihanouk received 90 per cent of the votes.

In the next election he proved an even better vote-getter when he polled 99 per cent of the votes cast. Since that time his domination of the government has been complete. He rules the party, the government, and the country as absolutely as any absolute monarch ever could. No important decisions of any kind have been made in the last fourteen years without his personal endorsement. Even though he gave up the crown officially, for every practical purpose he is the uncrowned king of the Khmers, and by his people he is treated as such.

CHAPTER 11

****

CAMBODIA
UNDER SIHANOUK

CAMBODIAN COURTIERS SHOW Sihanouk absolute deference, which he accepts as natural, while behaving himself with absolute democracy toward foreigners. His manner was shown clearly during a press conference he gave while on a state visit to Japan in 1955. Sihanouk is very conscious of his public image, and for this reason he is very easy to approach. He took a seat with the reporters. His Cambodian entourage did not sit in his presence. When it was necessary for any of them to address the prince, they bowed deeply and pressed their palms together in the traditional Khmer gesture of respect.

His interpreter explained that His Highness did not speak English and that reporters' questions would be translated and put

111

to him in French. Sihanouk listened to each question intently, leaning forward as if to hear better. He replied in French, and an interpreter translated his reply into English. When a question was controversial or held great interest for him, the procedure was different. He lifted his hand slightly, to stop the interpreter from repeating the question in French. Then speaking rapidly in English, Sihanouk answered the question directly, his alert round face mirroring his emotions as he spoke. (This seemed to contradict the statement that His Highness did not speak English. However, in his position a mistake could be costly. If the exact meaning of a word escaped him, a wrong reply would cause difficulty for him in the press and in international circles. For this reason, although he understands and speaks English, he prefers to make his replies in French which he speaks fluently. Yet, as has been seen, if he feels strongly about something, he is too impatient to wait for translation.) After the conference he mingled with the reporters, drinking a cocktail and making jokes.

At home he is just as approachable. It is not unusual to find him talking to villagers in an odd corner of his country as he seeks to uncover the roots of his country's problems. He still likes to ride, and an official Cambodian publication explaining the features of the country carries a photograph of the prince on a jumping horse.

His lifelong interest in music continues, and he still plays the piano and saxophone and composes his own music. In recent years he has taken an interest in moviemaking. In late 1968 he suddenly decided to stage an international film festival in Phnom Penh. Films were entered from thirty countries. One of the winners was "The Little Prince," with music, direction, and script by Prince Norodom Sihanouk. The star was his teen-age son.

At a nightclub party after the showings, Sihanouk took the microphone and sang several songs. The only American present was a United Press reporter who wrote: "He sang in French in a style somewhat between Dean Martin and vintage Bing Crosby."

Sihanouk likes to go on the radio and explain his actions to his people. He even explains things that would seem not to be any business of the public. For example, when his daughter divorced her husband, an outraged Sihanouk explained over the radio that it was not his fault, and that he thought his daughter behaved in a disgraceful manner.

The prince's official duties and title varies with his desires. Directly after his abdication, he became premier, with his father as head of state. When King Suramarit died in 1960, it posed a constitutional crisis. The Royal Council announced that it was unable to pick a successor, and the reasons were outlined by Sihanouk himself in a speech to the nation. He reminded the people that when he abdicated he swore never to take back the crown and explained that this left the Council with a choice of several hundred princes who were blood descendants of King Ang Duong and therefore eligible for the crown. Sihanouk went on to explain that it was impossible to make a choice because the followers of Son Ngoc Thanh were creating dissention among the eligibles. He accused Thanh's followers of doing this in order to start a civil war, which they would be able to use as an excuse for setting up a republic with Thanh as president.

When finally the situation could not be resolved, the Assembly —dominated by members of Sihanouk's party—passed a resolution asking the prince to assume the position of head of state without taking the crown. He accepted. Although he exercises the duties of head of state, his mother, Princess Kossamak, presides at royal social functions.

Although the kingdom is without a king, Sihanouk has said: "I am convinced in my heart that the Throne is still an indispensable institution in Cambodia." This statement seems at odds with his refusal to permit a king to be elected. It has been suggested, with good reason, that he does not want any other man elevated above himself. Yet no one can doubt Sihanouk's sincerity for renouncing the throne because he feels he can accomplish more as a political leader than he could as a monarch. Although he did permit his father's elevation, this was different. Suramarit was a quiet, unambitious man, content to let his dynamic son lead; another member of the royal family might not be so inclined. Factions which could lead to the dissention Sihanouk prophesized might grow up around the monarch. He has sons of his own, and it has been suggested that one of them be elected king. But Sihanouk has replied that under no circumstances would he permit one of his family to become king because he understands too well the frightful burden of the position. And so Cambodia has continued for ten years as a kingless kingdom ruled by an uncrowned king.

As the government is set up today, executive power is held by ministers in a form roughly comparable to government in France. The ministers are appointed by the head of state just as the premier appoints his cabinet.

There is also a unique assembly known as the Council of the Kingdom, which has twenty-four members. Two members of the Council are appointed by the king from princes of the royal family. Two additional members are elected by the National Assembly from among its members, eight are elected from the provinces, eight more come from representatives of the different professions, and four are appointed to represent the government ministers. The plan is that the Council will represent a cross section of the entire nation. Bills passed by the National Assembly go to the Council, but only for advice. If the Council disagrees, however, the Assembly must reconsider the bill.

Modern Cambodia is divided into fourteen provinces, each administered by a *chauvaykhet,* or provincial governor. Under him are districts comprised of a number of villages, or *khums;* the number varies, depending upon how widely separated the villages are. A *mekhum,* or headman, governs the *khum.*

Like Washington, D.C., Phnom Penh, the capital, is a district of its own. The city's name means "Hill of the Lady Penh," and there is a story connected with the name. Many years ago, at the place where the Mekong, Tonle Sap, and Brassaq rivers form a watery crossroads, a lady named Penh was trapped by flooding waters. She took refuge on a hill where the raging torrent had tossed an uprooted tree. Inside a hollow in the tree she found four small Buddhas. Associating this with the four "arms" of water formed by the Mekong entering and leaving the confluence with the Brassaq and Tonle Sap, she built a tiny shrine to hold the four Buddhas. The shrine grew in popularity and in time resulted in the giant golden spire that looks down on Phnom Penh today.

Norodom Street, the city's main thoroughfare, starts at the foot of the shrine hill and runs for two miles to a slender monument of lotus-bud design which honors the country's independence. Government buildings and homes of the wealthy are located in this elite area. The center of the city has a distinct French appearance, but on the outskirts the architecture is strictly old Khmer—that is, nipa-palm huts raised on stilts.

The location of Phnom Penh has always been highly desirable because of the transportation advantages of the rivers coming together at this point. However, the Khmers made no city here because of the terrific floods that come each year when the water begins to back up into the Tonle Sap River and into the Great Lake; their capital was at Oudong, twenty miles up the Tonle Sap. It was the French in 1867 who moved the capital to the present site because of transportation and shipping advantages. They began systematically to build a city, constructing concrete dikes to stop the flooding.

Phnom Penh has a population of about 150,000 Khmers. The next largest ethnic group is the Chinese with 100,000. Each group clings stubbornly to its own culture, which often includes native dress as well as custom. Western clothing is becoming more prominent, but one still sees Cambodians in *sampots,* a kind of sarong that is gathered up between the legs with the ends fastened to a belt. Indians appear in turbans and saris, and many Cham-Malays wear bag-pants reminiscent of *The Arabian Nights.* The Cham-Malays are Moslems and occasionally one is seen wearing a fez, which marks a person of distinction who has made the pilgrimage to the holy city of Mecca.

The royal palace is located near the river and is enclosed by a wall. The wall is in the traditional Khmer style, with a main gate that is topped by a golden spire. Beyond the wall are buildings that include the king's private residence, the throne room, the pagoda with its floor of solid silver, the royal museum, the Pavilion of the Sacred Sword where the Prah Khan is kept, and the open-air Pavilion of the Royal Dancers. There is also a royal stable for the horses Sihanouk loves to ride and for the sacred white elephant which he keeps as an ancient symbol of royalty. (White elephants are actually rare albinos and are a dirty pink rather than a true white.)

The royal *corps de ballet* preserves the ancient dances depicted by the carved *apsaras* (heavenly dancers) on the walls of Angkor. Unfortunately, the dancers perform only for Prince Sihanouk and his invited guests, although they make an occasional New Year's pilgrimage to Angkor. Here the girls dance in the evening by the light of flickering torches on the great causeway in front of Angkor Wat. This magnificent scene transports the beholder back to the days of Khmer greatness.

There is one major difference between the modern Khmer dancers and those carved on the walls of the lost city. The stone *apsaras* are scantily clad while the modern costumes are brilliantly elaborate and concealing. The reason is that today's costumes are Siamese instead of Khmer. When Angkor was sacked by the Siamese in the fifteenth century, the 4,000 dancing girls were taken back to Ayuthia, the Thai capital. Here the Buddhist king looked with disfavor on the scant, simple costumes and had new ones designed, using rich silk brocades and multitudes of jewels. These captive girls and their descendants carried on the Angkorean dance traditions, which evolved into the similar classical Thai dancing of today.

Cambodia made no attempt to keep the dance tradition alive, and as the years passed it was forgotten. Finally, two hundred years after the fall of Angkor, "Siamese" dancing was returned to the land of its birth. The royal ballet continued to be Siamese, employing Siamese dancers, until King Sisowath ordered the training of Cambodian girls in the early twentieth century. In his day the 200-

Classical dancing in the Khmer tradition has been kept alive by the Siamese since the fall of Angkor Thom.

girl *corps de ballet* was part of the royal harem he maintained in addition to his seventy-five wives. When he died, the king had one official wife for each year of his life.

The dances are very stylized, alternating between static poses and rapid movement. Since for centuries no new dances have been introduced, every movement has grown into a tradition. Each gesture must be done precisely as it has been done for the last several hundred years.

There are no male dancers in the Cambodian ballet. The male parts are taken by girls who wear men's costumes and masks. These girls begin training when they are eight years old. Their teachers are former dancers who rule their small charges like tyrants. The roles the girls learn, all based upon classical stories, are about princes, princesses, kings, gods, wicked demons, and—for comedy— monkey men. A typical play might be a fragment from the *Ramayana,* the famous Indian tale of Prince Rama and his adventures in search of his wife *Sita.* Aiding him is the monkey-king Hanuman. Other plays are based upon varying legends, but always tell of princesses in distress and the trials of handsome princes in rescuing them. The poorer classes are not represented in these plays.

CHAPTER 12

****

CAMBODIA AT PLAY AND AT WORK

PHNOM PENH HAS been called the city of holidays because the Khmers have fourteen major national holidays and innumerable lesser ones. In addition, the different racial groups in the country have their own holy and feast days. The democratic Cambodians joyously join in them all. They even celebrate Joan of Arc Day, a holiday observed by the French during the years of the protectorate.

The three biggest holidays are Tet, the Chinese New Year, in early January; Constitution Day in May; and—most colorful of all—the Water Festival in November. Other important holidays are the Plowing of the Holy Furrow at the beginning of the spring rice-planting season, the anniversary of Buddha's entrance into Nirvana in May, and the Feast of the Ancestors in late summer.

119

Tet combines the holiday characteristics of the western Christmas and the Oriental New Year. Children are given toys, gifts, and new clothes. Families visit each other and go out to watch parades. A special custom is the Tet tree, as familiar a sight in this season as the lily is at Easter time in the United States. The tree is a small flowering bush, and if it blooms during Tet, it means good luck for the rest of the year. The Tet trees are sold on the streets. Just before the holiday, those that appear ready to bloom command a premium price from customers who want to insure their good luck.

Constitution Day is the most serious of the year's celebrations. There are parades, demonstrations by the armed forces, speeches by officials, and marches by school children. The government makes a special effort to remind the people on this day that the Cambodian Constitution is a gift from Sihanouk to his people.

In November comes the Water Festival, a sort of elaborate thanksgiving that marks the end of the long rainy season, the coming fish harvest at Tonle Sap, and the beginning of a new planting cycle. As noted before, the Mekong River cannot handle the huge flow of water during the rainy season. The surplus flood therefore backs into the Tonle Sap River, reversing its flow and swelling the Great Lake into an inland sea. The flood sweeps across fields and forests, refertilizing the land, as the Nile does in Egypt. The depth of the water is amazing. Lawrence P. Briggs, historian and authority on the Angkorean period, tells of sailing on Tonle Sap at the height of the flood period. He said that in places they sailed past trees so inundated that only their top branches were visible above the level of the lake.

The Water Festival begins at the time the water reverses itself and starts to flow out of the Great Lake again. The festival's origin is so old that no memory of it remains even in Khmer folklore. It is probably rooted in pagan rites for a river god who was ancient when Kambu was young. The festival lasts for three days and three nights. All work stops in Phnom Penh and thousands flock to the city to see the show.

The ceremonies open when the king is purified by a sprinkling of sacred water carried from the river in a conch horn. Since, in Khmer eyes, the king is both the land and the people, this act purifies the country and all the sons of Kambu. Prince Sihanouk has not taken part in the purification ceremony since his abdication; his mother, Queen Kossamak, now presides. It is also a royal duty to cut the thong of leather stretched across the river, which symbolically frees the water so that it can flow back out of Tonle Sap.

The festival's highlight is the boat races. Individual villages build their own boats and train the rowers for weeks before the festival. Great honor comes to the village with the winning boat. During the first two days there are numerous contests between pairs of boats. Then at sunset on the last day all boats gather for a mass race that is the most exciting feature of the festival. The boats, which are dugout canoes hollowed from a single log, are rowed by as many as forty people. The boats are used only for training and for the annual race itself. The rest of the year they are housed in the village pagoda. Before the race they are re-decorated, and new eyes are painted on the prow in the Chinese manner so that the boat can come alive. With its gay decorations and upturned prow and stern, the boat looks remarkably like the war vessels seen on the wall of the Bayon at Angkor Thom.

For the final race, as many as a hundred boats mass behind a leather thong that the judges stretch across the river as a starting line. Then the official starter rows out. He teases the crowd and entrants by starting to cut the thong and then changing his mind. Finally, he severs the cord with a stroke of his sword. The boats streak forward, racing downstream to the finish line in front of the royal barge. After the winner is acclaimed, a conch shell of river water is carried to the queen who sprinkles it on her head in a repetition of the purification ceremony.

The final event of the festival comes after the boat race. Floats decorated with patterns of light sail down the river. Their fanciful designs reflect colored lights in the water. When they have passed, the crowds begin to disperse. The river has now been reopened and the water can flow out of the Tonle Sap. The fish can be harvested. Farmers can return to refertilized farms. The people and their land have been purified, and the cycle of life can begin for another year.

Another colorful but more restricted ceremony is the Plowing of the Holy Furrow to mark the beginning of rice planting in May. The ceremony is held inside the palace grounds. A square area is marked off and an altar erected in each corner. A "King of the Plow," representing the king, is chosen from those who live in the palace. He guides the plow as it is pulled by two oxen chosen for their perfection. Following behind the plowman is a girl who walks in the sacred furrow, scattering rice on either side. The oxen are then unhitched from their yoke and led to a row of bowls. If the cattle go to the one filled with rice, there will be a bountiful harvest.

The Cambodians love shows. Motion pictures are shown only in Phnom Penh, and many villagers have never seen one. The same is true of television. Radio is known in the back country, but few villagers actually own sets. Each pagoda has a radio, however, and the government depends upon these to get news and information to the people quickly. Officials know that the pagoda *bonze* pass along the broadcasts to their congregations.

The villagers see mostly "shadow plays" and classical dramas performed by wandering groups that are sponsored by the government. The shadow plays are created by moving cut-out figures in front of a lighted screen. This type of entertainment is very old and was probably brought to Cambodia from Java in the days of the Sailendra.

Another popular village pastime is dancing of the *lamthom*. It is best described as a combination of western dancing and classical Cambodian ballet. Although couples dance together, they do not touch each other. Like the Hawaiian hula, movements of the hands are very important in the *lamthom*.

Bicycle racing and soccer are two western sports that have become popular in Cambodia. Also, most of the city schools have basketball courts for use by the students.

The country's economy is based solidly on agriculture. Eighty per cent of the Khmers are farmers who till their plots of land in much the same manner as their ancestors have for the last thousand years. However, nearly all farmers become fishermen between crops.

Industry has not been developed to any great degree. The French established some rubber plantations, but had to employ Vietnamese labor. Timber is an important industry, but it is controlled by the Chinese. Cottage industries, where the work is done at home, are common. Families carrying on this type of work often develop wonderful skills in silversmithing, pottery making, weaving, and dyeing.

As in all Oriental countries, the marketplace is a vital, colorful part of community life. The largest of these is the central market in Phnom Penh. Almost a half-mile square, it is housed in a huge building that outwardly resembles a railroad station. Large as the market is, it cannot accommodate all who want to flock to it. Those who are unable to find room inside crouch on the sidewalks outside.

The market opens early. At sunup, the merchants begin to arrive, carrying their merchandise. Some pull heavy loads, such as pottery, in small carts. Others pack cloth on their backs. Girls carry baskets of fruit on their heads. Each market regular has an assigned place for which he or she pays a small rental fee. Merchandise includes nearly everything that is small enough to carry. There are even traveling restaurants which are generally run by old women who walk along with a wooden yoke across their shoulders. On one end, a charcoal brazier is suspended; on the other cooking utensils and food, which ranges from fried bananas and fish to small rice-flour cakes and noodles.

The big merchants have permanent stores in other parts of the city. These marketeers sell only what they can carry to market each day. They bargain with great gusto, and there is no set price for any item; no one expects to sell or buy without prolonged haggling. As in the days of Angkor, women are the sharpest bargainers.

In the commodity market and in international trade, Cambodia is in a very favorable position. Generally, she exports more than she imports. The country's most important export item is rice. Cash value of rice exports is about 900 million *riels,* which means that the annual value of Cambodia's rice exports is $30 million a year (there are about 30 *riels* to the American dollar).

Rubber is the next most valuable export item. Annual exports are about $15 million. Fish, pepper, timber, kapok, livestock, beans, tobacco, and palm sugar are other commodities Cambodia produces for the export market. The result is a very favorable trade balance.

The list of imports reveals the country's economic deficiencies and indicates where further development is needed. Cotton, silk, rayon, and other piece goods are the leading imports. Cambodia also is dependent upon foreign trade for metal products, petroleum, automobiles and parts, machinery, electrical apparatuses, medicines, dairy products, bicycles, wheat flour, chemical products, sugar, paper, and tires.

Just as the country has been slow to develop industry, it has also been slow to exploit its mining potential. There is some limited gold mining by hand methods in Kampong Thom province, but the yield is minor. Mining is a cooperative village venture. The ore is dug from an open pit, then carried in hampers to the top where girls crush it by hammering. The ore is then washed or hand picked to obtain the precious metal. All gold obtained is sold to the government, and profits are divided equally among the villagers. The government has shown no interest in opening any other possible gold fields. There are numerous traveler's tales about caches of hidden Khmer gold in the jungles which were supposedly hidden by the Angkoreans when the Siamese sacked the great city. These stories should not be dismissed as fiction. After all, Henri Mouhot refused to believe similar stories, and he eventually saw the four faces of Lokesvara smiling at him from the towers of Angkor.

CHAPTER 13

****

LIFE IN THE VILLAGES

UPON LEAVING PHNOM Penh, with its mixture of modern and ancient, one moves back in time. Life in the villages has changed little from the time when the Khmer kings of Angkor Thom ruled all of Southeast Asia.

The Khmer has always called himself "the child of the river." He stays as close to the "mother of waters" as he can, building his home near a stream as part of a group with his fellow man. During the day he walks out to his farm, but in the evening he always comes back to the river.

The average Cambodian rice village is small. There are rarely over 200 inhabitants. The houses are always raised on stilts of hardwood and thatched with nipa palm over frames of bamboo.

A young Cambodian girl carries bananas to early morning market.

Herding water buffalo is a boy's chore in this Cambodian rice village. The head scarf is protection against the sun.

Thus, they remain well above the flood that comes regularly every season. These villages, no matter how small, all have a *wat,* or place of worship, and a marketplace for buying and selling.

The markets are generally smaller versions of the great market in Phnom Penh. There is a covered roof in the center of the town with some stalls inside. The rest of the village merchants squat on the ground in their assigned places to haggle and bargain as they have done for centuries.

Under the old Khmer system every bit of land belonged to the king, but any farmer could use what he needed. When the tenant died or moved, the land reverted to the king; it was not the farmer's to sell or pass on to his children. In other words, the land belonged to the tenant as long as he farmed it or lived on it. The French tried to establish a system of private ownership. A system of land registration was set up, but few Cambodian farmers bothered to register. The land had always been there for anyone who wanted it and they saw no reason for the French plan, which they regarded with suspicion. As a result, Cambodian land ownership in rural areas is much as it has always been.

Unlike most of the Orient, farming is easy in Cambodia because there is no back-breaking fertilizing to keep the soil productive. The river does this job by overflowing each year to deposit a fertile silt.

The hard work comes during the planting season. The farmer and his team of water buffalo churn through the mud paddy to prepare the ground for rice. In some areas the grain can be sown by hand directly into the paddies; in others the sprouted shoots must be set in by hand, which is the more usual method in the Orient. When this back-breaking work is done, there is little to do but wait for the harvest. No other cultivation is necessary in Cambodia. Except for fishing, which the Cambodian does not consider work, farmers now have plenty of time to enjoy life in their villages.

The harvest again brings a flurry of hard work. The grain is cut and threshed by hand. The farmer and his older sons take the shocks and beat the heads against an inclined board to knock off the grains of rice. Later, the harvest is stored in clay pots for the family's use, and the surplus is sold.

Farming is a simple life that exactly suits the Khmer's temperament. He is perfectly content with such a life and resists any change. The government, backed by United States economic aid, once tried to show the farmers how to raise more rice per paddy by using modern methods. But the farmers could not understand why they should need a larger yield. Told by a farm economist that it was his patriotic duty to grow more for king and country, one farmer replied: "I have enough for my family. I have seen the king and he looks well fed, so he must have enough too. Why bother with more?"

The Khmers are the best-fed people in the Orient. They eat two meals a day—breakfast at ten in the morning and supper at about five in the evening. A typical meal might be a rice ball, dried or fresh fish, and some *prahoc,* a highly spiced, fermented fish. This fish is an important staple in the Khmer diet, and part of the great Tonle Sap fish harvest is used to make this popular paste. Supplementing this basic diet are all kinds of fruits, from papaya to bananas, and often chicken, pork, and eggs. Tea is the favorite drink.

The villagers eat on the floor, sitting on woven mats. Clay bowls hold the food, which is usually cooked outside in an iron pot. Most activity is outside in the yard, and the house is used mainly for eating and sleeping. The homes, consisting usually of only one or two rooms, are sparsely furnished. Beds are seldom seen, since people sleep on mats, although some homes have raised platforms for sleeping.

The rice village is a happy place for children. Those under twelve have few chores. Their day consists of swimming in the streams, fishing in the rivers and rice paddies, and frolicking with friends. They go to the pagoda school usually only long enough to learn to read and write and to acquire moral and religious values. For many years a pagoda schooling was all the formal education that Cambodian children received. Since independence, more and more schools are being built in rural areas. Unfortunately, there is a lack of teachers. Many of those who teach in the remote areas have gone no farther in their own education than the equivalent of grammar school in the United States.

Scant schooling is a basic reason why Cambodia has little literature. Very few books are produced. Most of those that are written have a socialistic viewpoint. Newspapers, unless subsidized, do not have enough readers to survive on circulation alone. Although they do not care much for reading, Cambodians of all ages love stories. The tradition of folk tales is still very much alive, and the people never tire of hearing them over and over.

A particular favorite is the tale about a lady who wept because she had so many misfortunes. She poured out her misery to Buddha who told her that these miseries would go away if she would obtain a seed from a house that had never known sorrow. The next week Buddha found her singing happily. When the Enlightened One asked if she had found the Seed of Happiness, the old woman replied, "No, Blessed One. I went to every house seeking it and found no house that had not known sorrow. Every where I went I saw troubles much worse than my own, and from this I learned that I do not have it bad at all!"

Another folk tale is of a little girl who carelessly dropped a grain of rice. A *gecho*—the familiar house lizard—grabbed it. A cat saw the lizard and pounced on it. This brought out an angry dog. The cat's owner started to beat the dog, which infuriated the dog's owner. The two started to fight, and soon their families and then their neighbors joined in until everyone was fighting. Word reached Angkor that a fight was raging. The king thought it must be an attack by a foreign enemy and rushed out with ten thousand men and elephants. The king of neighboring Siam thought the Khmers were mobilizing to attack his country. He rushed out with his own troops and all because a careless little girl dropped a grain of rice, a war broke out.

Such stories are intended to entertain and teach a moral, and apparently the story-telling lessons work. Cambodia has an extremely low juvenile delinquency rate, although the average Khmer family is reluctant to punish its children. When a child's conduct is so bad that it warrants a whipping, he is usually spanked on the wrist or behind. A Cambodian child is never slapped; the head, as the seat of reason, is sacred. Even a friendly pat on the head is never seen among these people. Instead of whippings, Cambodian parents try to teach by example and through the moral teachings of the *bonze.*

When boys reach the age of twelve, they go with their fathers and older brothers to work in the fields. While they learn the secrets of cultivation, the girls at home are learning household tasks. A very important part of a young Cambodian girl's training is accompanying her mother to market. She squats silently beside the older woman and watches every gesture and listens to every word.

The father is the head of the family, but the mother is not the near-slave that she is in so many Oriental cultures. She is a partner in the family and knows her rights. Under Khmer law a man can have as many wives as he can afford, but few can afford more than one. However, if there are other wives the First Wife is the overseer of the others. There is a curious arrangement whereby the first woman a man marries may not be designated First Wife; it is understood from the beginning that she will be the number two wife. This can occur when a man is bethrothed to a girl too young to marry. For social or financial reasons her family will not permit the marriage unless she will be First Wife. In such a case there would be an understanding with the family of any woman he married prior to the wedding with the younger girl that the position of First Wife would go to the bride of the later wedding. A situation like this could only occur in the upper levels of society.

Cambodians try to limit their families to five children, which they consider the ideal number that can be cared for properly. All Cambodians, except Buddhist monks, are expected to marry. Bachelors and old maids are viewed with great disapproval. If a man or woman is not married by the time he or she is twenty-five, he is considered an insult to his family.

In the cities, western-style courtships are becoming more common. In the villages, however, marriages continue to be arranged, as they have been for cenutries. Courtship, such as it is, is a family matter. The mother or grandmother will open the matter by suggesting to her counterpart in another family that a union between the two families *might* be desirable.

Generally, it is considered more polite for the boy's family to open negotiations. If the girl's mother says cautiously that she does not know, this is the signal for further negotations. However, if she says her daughter is too young (even though the girl may be approaching "old-maid" status), then it is understood that she disapproves of a connection between the two families. But if the situation looks promising, the two grandmothers meet as often as possible. Squatting on the ground, their close-cropped hair makes them look like two old men discussing the rice crop (the older women cut their hair in the style of the men).

The traditional bargaining ability of Cambodian women is brought into play as each tries to find out the defects of the other's relatives. This bargaining is serious. It is considered a parental duty to provide a good and suitable marriage for one's children. Those who do not do so are held in contempt by their neighbors. As a result, courtship by proxy proceeds with caution and reserve.

Theoretically, the choice of a mate is made by the parents. However, if a young girl whispers, "Mama, get me that nice young man with whom I danced the *lamthon* at the festival!" Mama does the best she can, provided she considers the young man suitable.

Once the engagement is announced, the groom-to-be goes to work for his future wife's family for a time set by mutual agreement. The boy tries to make it as short as possible and the family tries to make it as long as possible because the labor is free. During this trial work period, the young man is little more than a slave. Supposedly, this permits the family to see what kind of character he has and how industrious he is. It has happened that the young man has become so enraged at his treatment by the family that he breaks off the engagement. It has been said that the frequent harsh premarital treatment is the major reason why no self-respecting Cambodian son-in-law will live with his wife's family after marriage. He wants to get away from them as quickly as possible.

After he serves his free-work period, there is still another requirement to fulfill before the wedding. He must build a house for his prospective bride. This is no great problem; he has only to find unoccupied land, clear it of trees, and build a dike to hold irrigation water for his paddy and join it to a nearby stream.

The wedding is a two-day festival, beginning with a procession of guests bearing gifts. The wedding date is always a lucky one, for the groom has consulted an astrologer who, with the aid of a *bonze,* picks the date that is the most fortuitous for a wedding. At a precise moment determined by the stars, the bride and groom kneel before the altar while the *bonze* performs the religious ceremony. The young people wear rented garments that simulate the costume of ancient Khmer kings and queens. At the conclusion of the ceremony, the hands of the couple are tied together with red silk thread. Seeds are thrown over them, just as in America rice is thrown at newlyweds. Following the tying ceremony, the couple are given instructions in getting along with each other and in the duties of husband and wife.

After this comes a most important part of the wedding. A bowl is placed at the door, and all the quests drop money into it as they depart. A wedding is expensive, and the poor groom cannot possibly pay for it. So the guests, who have had a wonderful time, are expected to pay for their part of the fun. The groom never recovers enough to pay all his bills, but every bit dropped into the wedding bowl helps.

CHAPTER 14

****

THE BONZE

BECAUSE ALL YOUNG men must take the robe for a certain period
of time, the most familiar sight in Cambodia is the brightly garbed
bonze walking slowly along the byways of the country. The monk
in his saffron mantle shaded by his parasol may therefore be a
prince of the realm or the son of the poorest man in the kingdom.

The Cambodian boy becomes associated with the *bonze* very
early in life. He is taken to the pagoda by his father and turned
over to the monks for training, which will continue in some form
until he is sixteen. At that time, as part of entering manhood the
student must himself become a *bonze* for about six months to a
year.

The boy's initiation into the priesthood begins with an ancient

The umbrella shades the shaven head of the monk.

ritual in which the novice wears very rich clothes in imitation of Buddha who was a prince before he renounced the material world to become a penniless, wandering teacher. After this ritual, the novice puts on the simple saffron robe of the monk. All hair is shaved from his body, and his head will continue to be shaved as long as he wears the robe.

During his time as a *bonze*, the young Khmer possesses nothing but his robe, his parasol to protect his shaven pate from the sun, and his begging bowl. He is dependent entirely upon charity. He is not even permitted to till the soil, for he is liable to kill worms in the ground, which would violate the first tenet of conduct, not to kill.

The monks usually live in huts or buildings adjoining the main pagoda. They are located under a tree, ordinarily a *banyan*, in imitation of Buddha who lived under such a tree. He arises before dawn, and his first hours are spent in meditation and prayer before a statute of Buddha. He then sets out with his begging bowl to seek his only meal of the day. He will walk the streets until someone takes pity on him and gives him some food. Professional monks usually have certain families who feed them regularly as a means of gaining merit. In contrast to other Buddhist countries (Japan, for instance) there are no fat monks in Cambodia, in fact, there is an adage in the country: "Lean as a monk's belly." The filled bowls are taken back to the pagoda where all the monks eat together. The food, once it is obtained, must be consumed before noon.

In the afternoon the *bonze* may study, teach in the pagoda schools, give assistance to people, or meditate. He is not permitted to do any other type of work. He is also prohibited from engaging in politics, but this restriction is not rigidly observed by higher-ranking monks. A high Buddhist is said to be an influential adviser to Prince Sihanouk. One of the greatest sins is to kill or do harm to a *bonze*. However, if attacked himself, the monk is not permitted to make a complaint. He lives in a world completely removed from ordinary people.

Each pagoda is headed by a head *bonze* known as a *chau-atikar*. All other monks, novices, and students come under his direction. He in turn is responsible to the head *bonze* of the province who answers to top church officials in Phnom Penh. These officials are responsible to the king who is the titular head of the religion.

After a young man serves his obligatory time as a priest, he returns to his former life. However, if he prefers the monastic life, he can remain as a professional monk. There are in Cambodia today more than 75,000 professional monks and over 3,000 monasteries. In addition there are about 25,000 novices, bringing the total of monks to around 100,000 in a nation of 5 million people.

One cannot understand the curious life of the *bonze* without a knowledge of his religion and what it means to the Cambodian. As mentioned earlier, 90 per cent of Cambodia follows the Little Vehicle—or Hinayana—sect of Buddhism. It teaches that life is basically unhappy and that this sorrow is caused by desire. Desire in this case means hungering after anything, be it wealth, food, or ambition. The sorrow of life can be overcome only by crushing this desire. Although the true Hinayana Buddhist reveres the Buddha, or Enlightened One, as an ideal he would like to emulate, he has no gods to whom he can pray for help and moral guidance. Man, he believes, controls his own destiny by the power of his will. His life does not end with his death. Rather, his soul is reborn through reincarnation, and this cycle of life is repeated endlessly until he becomes enlightened. Then, as a Buddha, he enters Nirvana and becomes a part of the spirit of creation.

The Hinayana Buddhist believes that every deed in this life is reflected in the next life. If he observes all the commandments and acquires much "merit," he may be born to a high station—even as high as king. On the other hand, a bad life now can condemn him to rebirth as a dog or lower animal in the next life, and neither heaven nor providence nor luck can influence this fate. His fortunes and misfortunes arise from the life he led before.

The Buddhist moral code is set by ten tenets of conduct which some western writers compare to the Ten Commandments, to which, in some cases, they are parallel:

1. You shall not kill life in any form.
2. You shall not steal.
3. You must be chaste.
4. You will not lie.
5. You must avoid intoxicants.
6. You are to eat only at the sanctioned hour.
7. You must avoid any activity that excites the senses.
8. Shun personal adornments. [This even includes perfume and powder.]
9. You will not sleep in a raised bed.
10. Avoid handling money or touching gold.

The first five laws are mandatory for all Buddhists, but the *bonze* must keep all ten. Few of the general public are able to keep the commandments. However, the troubles that arise from such a fall from grace can be partially offset by achieving merit, and one can amass merit by doing good deeds.

A curious thing about Buddhism is that it is not at odds with other religions, as long as the other religions do not try to stifle Buddhism. For centuries Sivaism, Brahmanism, and Buddhism were practiced side by side without conflict. Buddhism does not dispute the people's belief in the supernatural and in animism. It is not at all unusual to see a Cambodian leave the pagoda after making his devotions to Buddha and then slip away to a tiny home-made shrine where he offers rice to a *neak ta,* or spirit. These spirits are everywhere—in trees, rice paddies, mountains, and even rivers. The Buddhist religion in Cambodia recognizes these spirits and what they mean to the people. Monks are often called to exorcise these nature spirits when they prove harmful. Another surviving Khmer superstition is the use of amulets, or *katha.* They can be bought either from the village sorcerer or from stores.

The French were careful to preserve the centuries-old traditions of the people. The Hinayana concept of accepting life as one found it and shunning change exactly suited the French colonial policy.

Today, with the French gone, changes are coming about, and some of these changes are bound to attack the foundation of Buddhism as it is practiced in Cambodia.

Criticism of the religious order is growing in the cities. In every case it comes from young people and is a result of increased education. The students profess to be repelled by superstitious elements they claim to see in Buddhism. They also complain about the *bonze*. Since the monks are not permitted to do any work other than teaching, they must be fed, and their beggar existence is a severe drain on the national economy. The country, the students say, supports 100,000 non-productive men.

The students also cast doubt on the religious sincerity of many of the 70,000 professional monks. They claim that although many monks may be sincere, others take the robe only because they are too lazy to work. In some instances these charges against the *bonze* have been traced to Communist sources. The Buddhists have traditionally resisted any kind of change, social or moral, and their influence with the Khmers is a bar to the expansion of Communist ideas in Cambodia.

In any case, the bulk of Cambodians still respect the men of the robe. The intellectuals who criticize them are still too small a group to make a difference. But the criticism will undoubtedly increase as higher education becomes more common.

CHAPTER 15

THE HILL PEOPLE

FOR SOME REASON, buried deep in their ancestral history, the Khmers have always clung to the lowland, shunning the hill country. The high ground has been left to the *phnongs,* as the Khmers term all the various primitive tribes who live in the timbered, mountainous regions of the Moi Plateau and the Dangrek Hills.

Phnong means savage, and to call a Khmer a *phnong* is the height of insult. The social division between the *phnongs* and the Khmers goes back in history so far that its origin has been forgotten. We know that it existed in Angkorean days because Chou Ta-kuan tells us that the Khmers made slaves of these savages from the hill country. The *phnongs'* slaves were considered so lowly that they were not permitted to live in houses but made to sleep on the ground with the cattle and pigs.

The relationship between the two peoples is curious because no real caste system has ever existed in Cambodia. While accepting Indian laws and culture, the Khmers rejected the Hindu caste system. Therefore, it is strange that they draw so firm a line between themselves and the hill people, and it is even stranger that the sharp division survives to this day. The separation cannot be explained on the basis of differences in nationality or ethnic background. Although the idea infuriates a Cambodian, ethnologists insist that the Khmers and the *phnongs* are identical people.

It is not known when the cultures of the Khmers and the *phnongs* separated. It may have happened when the Hindus first arrived in Indochina. The *phnongs* may be descendants of those natives who resisted the imposition of Hindu laws and culture. The latter withdrew to the hills to continue their old way of life while the natives of the lowland were quickly Indianized by the Hindu invaders who came in the first century A.D.

Even today the people of the highlands remain animists, believing that all things in nature have souls. They believe wholeheartedly that spirits and demons live in rocks, trees, and even in the wind. They are, as a result, very superstitious and fearful of the spirit world that surrounds them. If they cut down a tree, the spirit inside would destroy the woodsmen unless the spirit could be placated. The same is true if they move a rock, grow rice, or even eat a piece of fruit. This belief results in great power for the village sorcerer whose benevolent spells are the people's only weapon against these evil spirits.

Unlike minority groups in other countries, the despised *phnongs* have no desire to be integrated with the Khmers. They are entirely satisfied with their primitive life and fiercely resist any attempts at change. They refuse to acknowledge the authority of the Cambodian government. They regard themselves as free men and live in the highland jungles, beholden to no one but their village chief and their sorcerer. The Cambodian government in turn leaves them strictly alone. Both are content with this arrangement.

Although the Cambodians classify all hill people as savages, there are actually a dozen different individual tribes and these seem to be split between two definite racial groups. One group, lighter in skin color and larger in stature than the other, is Indonesian in type. The second group, darker and with woolly hair, is more Negroid.

All the tribes, for the most part, live a nomadic life. Like the lowlanders, they build their villages on stilts. But life varies from tribe to tribe. Some maintain individual homes. Others live in communal long-houses like those seen in Polynesia. Some of these long-houses are said to be as much as 300 feet long. Rooms are partitioned with bamboo for individual families, with bachelors living in a central communal room. Here, as in the rest of Cambodia, bachelorhood is frowned upon. Each man is expected to be a husband and a father by the time he is twenty-five. Spinsterhood is unthinkable. If there is a shortage of husbands, plurality of wives solves the problem.

Life in these villages is completely communal. Everything belongs to the tribe except the weapons a man carries. These are generally a knife with a curved blade like a Malay *kris,* javelins, and bows and arrows. The *phnongs* live by hunting, gathering fruits, and growing rice. They are too far upland to benefit from the Mekong's annual refertilization of the valley's rice paddies, so they use the cut-and-burn method to cultivate their land. When the soil is exhausted, the entire village moves on. Here the jungle is cleared and the debris burned to open land for new farms. This cycle continues, with the tribes migrating slowly over the years.

Only one of the tribes, the Kuoy of the Dangrek Mountains, has had much contact with the lowland Khmers. Many of the Kuoy have come down to the valley to work and sometimes to marry. The other tribes maintain their age-old isolation and loyalty to pre-Hindu customs and gods.

****

CHAPTER 16

CAMBODIA AND THE MODERN WORLD

THE SPREAD OF communism in Asia has changed Cambodia from a country of slight importance in the international world to one of increasing prominence. Most Asian observers are convinced that this little country will be the next arena of confrontation between East and West.

Cambodia is also aware of the danger she faces in the squeeze between these two forces. The belligerent and often stubborn foreign policies of Prince Sihanouk's government are solidly based on his fear of being dominated by either side.

As far as the average Cambodian is concerned, his world is small. It encompasses his own country and his immediate neighbors, Laos, Vietnam, and Thailand. He has never worried much about the Laotians, but he hates the Vietnamese and constantly quarrels with the Thais. Every Cambodian, from prince to peasant, is convinced that these two traditional enemies are only waiting for a chance to dismember the land of the Khmers, as they have tried to do in the past.

The Khmers refuse to believe that times have changed. In talking with Cambodians, their individual opinions all tend to the collective view that Cambodia still must fight for its existence. One hears them complain that it was only a little more than sixty years ago that the Thais occupied two Cambodia provinces and even claimed Angkor. Prince Sihanouk has pointed this out himself and angrily added, "To this very day the Vietnamese rule over a third of our country and a half-million of our people."

The latter claim refers to the rich Mekong delta which France ceded to Vietnam. At the Geneva Conference in 1954, Sihanouk announced that he would continue to press for its return. He made a similar statement during a later state visit to the Philippines. All this was noted with alarm in Saigon. The Vietnamese know that the abundant rice from the Mekong delta is necessary to their country's survival as a nation.

Cambodia's hatred of Vietnam is the reason for Sihanouk's cooperation with Vietnam's enemies. Time and again the prince has been accused of cooperating with the Communists who are fighting against South Vietnam. Viet Minh guerrilla bands lurk around the Cambodian border, strike quickly at Vietnamese points, then fade back into the sanctuary of Cambodia's jungles. Between 1963 and 1969 there were many charges that Sihanouk was permitting supplies and munitions for the Communist-led North Vietnam army to pass regularly through Cambodia. Sihanouk flatly denied the allegations, claiming his country was completely neutral. "When two elephants fight," he said, "the wise ant stands to one side to avoid being tromped."

The United States view of Cambodia in this period was set forth in some "Background Notes," issued by the U.S. Department of State: "This [Cambodia's neutrality policy] has resulted in a markedly expanded relations with the Communist bloc."

After Cambodia won its independence from France, Sihanouk, anxious to build up his country's military strength, accepted American aid. His decision was not popular in government circles. There was a fear—shared by Sihanouk himself—that it would be difficult to accept American aid without losing Cambodia's newly won independence. Into this uncertain situation, the Chinese Communists moved swiftly to show friendliness to Cambodia. Sihanouk was invited to make a state visit to China. He was hosted by dictator Mao Tse-tung and president Chou En-lai.

After his return to Cambodia Sihanouk made a speech in the General Assembly in which he said: "We will accept aid from the right, from the left and from the center in any way that will assist our country." He went on again to demand that Vietnam return the Mekong delta. At the same time he angrily rejected the United States suggestion that he join SEATO, the Southeast Asia Treaty Organization, to present a solid military front against Communist aggression. The Philippines, Vietnam, Malaya, and Thailand are members.

Although Sihanouk denounced what he called American attempts to pressure him, he continued to accept U.S. aid between 1955 and 1963. According to the U.S. State Department, the United States gave Cambodia $309.6 million in economic aid and an additional $83.7 million in direct military assistance. This aid took the form of assisting the armed forces, stabilizing the national economy, and financing projects in education, agriculture, public administration, and health. Despite glowing reports, much of this aid was unsuccessful. The Cambodian does not want to change his age-old ways of growing rice, he is satisfied with his health, and he has no desire to develop industries.

As part of its aid, the United States constructed a 130-mile highway through the jungle to connect Phnom Penh with the new port of Sihanoukville on the Gulf of Siam. At last reports, the road is breaking up, shifting foundations and the encroachment of the jungle is destroying it. American building methods are blamed for the deterioration. But the real reason for the trouble is probably lack of proper maintenance.

Sihanouk gradually became disgruntled over U.S. aid and what he considered American attempts to dictate to him. He abruptly refused all U.S. assistance in 1963, breaking off diplomatic relations at the same time. He then accepted four Soviet MIG aircraft and increased aid from Communist China. But the United States did not interpret this action as a solid Cambodian move into the Communist camp. The State Department "Background Notes" said: "Prince Sihanouk has on numerous occasions in the past denounced Communism, pointing out that democracies provide liberties for the individual, while Communism suppresses individual liberties."

In a speech, Sihanouk once said, "We know perfectly well that the Reds only applaud our neutrality because it serves their interest." Despite this statement, Sihanouk continued to be friendly with Red China. In doing so, he felt he was serving the best interests of Cambodia. It was the age-old Cambodian trick of playing one enemy against the other—not that the prince considered the United States as such an enemy. The U.S. is, however, a friend of Cambodia's traditional enemies, Vietnam and Thailand. Of the two, Cambodia fears Vietnam most. The build-up of that country by the United States as part of the Vietnamese war made Sihanouk nervous. A strong Vietnam has always meant trouble for Cambodia.

Attempts to convince the prince that this is not true are met with the complaint that Vietnam still holds a half-million Khmers in "captivity" in the Mekong delta. In Sihanouk's view, any blow to Vietnam is an aid to the future security of Cambodia. One way of adding to Vietnam's misfortune was to permit supplies for the Viet Cong to funnel through Cambodia to the Communist guerrillas. Reports of Communist munitions movements through Cambodia became so strong in 1967 that international observers were convinced that Sihanouk was moving totally into the Red China orbit. They felt that the prince was convinced that South Vietnam could not win even with powerful American aid. It appeared that he was protecting Cambodia from possible Chinese fury when the Reds took over all of Vietnam.

Then, suddenly in 1968, the unpredictable prince pulled another surprise. He closed the country to foreign newspapermen. The official curtain was so tight that even diplomats did not know what was going on inside Cambodia. A Los Angeles *Times* reporter, writing from the international listening post in Hong Kong, said: "A gigantic pipeline through Cambodia supplying the Viet Cong with arms, ammunition, food and medicine—operated with the cooperation of senior Cambodian officials—appears to be blowing up into a major political crisis."

Very little news has leaked out of Cambodia. With his complete control of the country, Sihanouk is able to keep official secrets well buried. It is known that, acting on his orders, five top government officials were arrested. One was the leftist Chao Seng, a man who had but recently returned from a Sihanouk-imposed exile from Cambodia. His arrest indicated that the prince now feared that he had gone too far in aiding the Communist cause. This sudden anti-Communist move was in keeping with his policy of favoring first one side, then the other.

The United States has kept a careful watch over developments in Cambodia and has been anxious to re-establish relations with the strategically placed country. The visit to Cambodia of the former Jacqueline Kennedy, widow of the late President John F. Kennedy, was viewed by newspapers as a step to regain Sihanouk's good will. Mrs. Kennedy denied that there was anything official in her trip. She traveled under auspices of the U.S. State Department, however, and Sihanouk treated her like visiting royalty. At the time of her visit several American servicemen were interned in Phnom Penh for allegedly violating Cambodian neutrality. Not long after Mrs. Kennedy's visit they were released.

The next year Sihanouk reversed his previous position, when he denied that Viet Cong forces were operating from Cambodia against South Vietnam. After the U.S. charge that the 1969 spring offensive by the Viet Cong was staged from Cambodia's Svay Rieng province, Sihanouk said in a speech that he would not object to the United States bombing Communist military camps in his country. He qualified the statement by asserting that he knew of no such targets. However, his speech indicated a further withdrawal from Communist rapport.

Then, in April, 1969, he issued a formal statement that he would resume diplomatic relations with the United States. The announcement followed a United States statement that it "recognized the sovereignty, independence, neutrality and territorial integrity of Cambodia within its present frontiers." Within a few days Sihanouk reversed himself again, complaining that the U.S. statement did not mention certain islands in the Gulf of Siam. Then, in late June, the matter was straightened out. The prince announced that Cambodia and the United States would exchange *chargés d'affaires,* which is one step below exchange of ambassadors and full diplomatic recognition.

Where will this lead? No one is optimistic enough to predict that it means permanent alignment of Cambodia with the West. Sihanouk is expected to move in whatever direction he feels is best for his country. In every way, he represents modern Cambodia. With his enormous personal popularity and youth (he is under fifty) he is sure to dominate his country's politics for a long time to come. Internal opposition to him is minor. Although his schools are turning out young people who are dissatisfied with his slowness in solving Cambodia's social problems, this opposition is not expected to reach serious proportions in the prince's lifetime.

So, on the international front, Cambodia will continue to maintain its neutrality and fight to hold its independence. On the domestic front Sihanouk's policy is for improved education for the Khmers and a gradual modernization of his country. He has said that his wish is to recreate in Cambodia a nation of which the old kings of Angkor would be proud.

Then when it appeared that the political situation in Cambodia was stabilized events took a surprising turn. On March 19, 1970, while Sihanouk was in France on a vacation, Lieutenant General Lon Nol, the defense minister, and Sisowath Sirik Matak, Sihanouk's cousin, seized control of the government. The two conspirators immediately announced Sihanouk's ouster as Head of State. They blamed Sihanouk for collaboration with the Viet Cong and with poor economic policies which hampered Cambodia's growth. Sihanouk immediately left for Moscow to seek aid for his cause.

As this book went to press Lon Nol asked the United Nations for help in maintaining Cambodia's neutrality. At the same time Sihanouk in Moscow announced that he was organizing a resistance movement to fight his enemies in Cambodia. Civil war seems inevitable. However, with Lon Nol in complete command of Cambodia's army, Sihanouk can expect support only from the rural dwellers who still look upon him as king. These followers lack the equipment and training to fight a civil war. So Sihanouk must have help from Russia and Red China to wage a successful fight to return to power. If the prince fails to get this support, those who know him think he will go into exile, but this exile will last only until he sees an opportunity to strike back at his enemies. He is a tough, bitter fighter who will never give up completely. For the Khmers of Cambodia all this foreshadows long years of struggle and strife.

BIBLIOGRAPHY

Casey, Robert J. *The Four Faces of Siva*. Indianapolis, 1929.

Gosh, Manomehan. *A History of Cambodia*. Saigon, 1960.

Krasa, Miloslav. *Temples of Angkor*. London, 1963.

Leonowens, Anna. *An English Governess at the Siamese Court*. London, 1870.

MacDonald, Malcolm. *Angkor*. London, 1959.

Parmentier, Henri. *Angkor*. Saigon, 1955.

U.S. State Department. *Background Notes: Cambodia*. Washington, 1965.

INDEX

*NOTE: *Italic entries indicate illustrations.*